The Wiersbe
BIBLE STUDY SERIES

The **Wiersbe**
BIBLE STUDY SERIES

EZEKIEL

Bowing

Before Our

Awesome God

David C Cook®

transforming lives together

THE WIERSBE BIBLE STUDY SERIES: EZEKIEL
Published by David C Cook
4050 Lee Vance View
Colorado Springs, CO 80918 U.S.A.

David C Cook Distribution Canada
55 Woodslee Avenue, Paris, Ontario, Canada N3L 3E5

David C Cook U.K., Kingsway Communications
Eastbourne, East Sussex BN23 6NT, England

The graphic circle C logo is a registered trademark of David C Cook.

All Scripture quotations in this study are taken from the Holy Bible, New
International Version®, NIV®. Copyright © 1973, 1984 by Biblica, Inc.™ Used by
permission of Zondervan. All rights reserved worldwide. www.zondervan.com.

In the *Be Reverent* excerpts, unless otherwise noted, all Scripture quotations are taken
from the King James Version of the Bible. (Public Domain.) Scripture quotations
marked NKJV are taken from the New King James Version®. Copyright © 1982 by
Thomas Nelson, Inc. Used by permission. All rights reserved; NIV are taken from the
Holy Bible, New International Version®, NIV®. Copyright © 1973, 1984 by Biblica,
Inc.™ Used by permission of Zondervan. All rights reserved worldwide. www.zondervan.
com; and NASB are taken from the New American Standard Bible®, Copyright © 1960,
1995 by The Lockman Foundation. Used by permission. (www.Lockman.org.)

All excerpts taken from *Be Reverent*, second edition, published by David C
Cook in 2010 © 2000 Warren W. Wiersbe, ISBN 978-1-4347-0050-6.

ISBN 978-0-7814-1038-0
eISBN 978-1-4347-0859-5

© 2014 Warren W. Wiersbe

The Team: Karen Lee-Thorp, Amy Konyndyk, Nick Lee, Jack
Campbell, Helen Macdonald, Karen Athen
Series Cover Design: John Hamilton Design
Cover Photo: iStockphoto

Printed in the United States of America
First Edition 2014

1 2 3 4 5 6 7 8 9 10

082714

Contents

Introduction to Ezekiel

A Lack

One thing that is lacking in the church today is a sincere reverence for the name and glory of the Lord. At least a dozen times in the book of Psalms you find the psalmist praising God's holy name. In fact, God's people are identified in Scripture as those who reverence God's name (Rev. 11:18).

Associated with God's name is God's glory, for His name is a glorious name (1 Chron. 29:13). When God's people glorify Him, they bring honor to His name, just as obedient children bring honor to their family name. "Hallowed be your name" is the first petition in the Lord's Prayer (Matt. 6:9), and one of the reasons God answers prayer is that His name might be glorified.

And an Answer

The messages of the prophet Ezekiel focus on the glory of God, the throne of God, and the honor of God's name. God is called "Lord GOD" (or "Sovereign LORD") over four hundred times in this book, and you find the solemn phrase "I am the LORD" fifty-nine times. In all that God says and does, He has one purpose in mind: "You will know that I am the LORD" (Ezek. 6:7).

When Ezekiel lived, spoke, and wrote his book, the Jewish people were captives in Babylon, and Ezekiel was there with them. He was not only a servant sent to speak to his people, but also a sign to the people (Ezek. 24:24, 27). God asked him to do many unusual things in order to get the attention of the people so they would hear the word of God. His spoken messages and his "sign messages" were both needed because the people had blind eyes and hard hearts. Ezekiel was a master of metaphor and imagery.

Is the prophecy of Ezekiel a book that's needed today? The eminent Jewish writer Elie Wiesel said, "No generation could understand Ezekiel as well—as profoundly—as ours." One thing is sure: Our generation *needs* the message of Ezekiel, for we are a people who lack the reverence we should have for the glory of God and the name of God.

—*Warren W. Wiersbe*

How to Use This Study

This study is designed for both individual and small-group use. We've divided it into eight lessons—each references one or more chapters in Warren W. Wiersbe's commentary *Be Reverent* (second edition, David C Cook, 2010). While reading *Be Reverent* is not a prerequisite for going through this study, the additional insights and background Wiersbe offers can greatly enhance your study experience.

The **Getting Started** questions at the beginning of each lesson offer you an opportunity to record your first thoughts and reactions to the study text. This is an important step in the study process as those "first impressions" often include clues about what it is your heart is longing to discover.

The bulk of the study is found in the **Going Deeper** questions. These dive into the Bible text and, along with helpful excerpts from Wiersbe's commentary, help you examine not only the original context and meaning of the verses but also modern application.

Looking Inward narrows the focus down to your personal story. These intimate questions can be a bit uncomfortable at times, but don't shy away from honesty here. This is where you are asked to stand before the mirror of God's Word and look closely at what you see. It's the place to take a good look at yourself in light of the lesson and search for ways in which you can grow in faith.

Going Forward is the place where you can commit to paper those things you want or need to do in order to better live out the discoveries you made in the Looking Inward section. Don't skip or skim through this. Take the time to really consider what practical steps you might take to move closer to Christ. Then share your thoughts with a trusted friend who can act as an encourager and accountability partner.

Finally, there is a brief **Seeking Help** section to close the lesson. This is a reminder for you to invite God into your spiritual-growth process. If you choose to write out a prayer in this section, come back to it as you work through the lesson and continue to seek the Holy Spirit's guidance as you discover God's will for your life.

Tips for Small Groups

A small group is a dynamic thing. One week it might seem like a group of close-knit friends. The next it might seem more like a group of uncomfortable strangers. A small-group leader's role is to read these subtle changes and adjust the tone of the discussion accordingly.

Small groups need to be safe places for people to talk openly. It is through shared wrestling with difficult life issues that some of the greatest personal growth is discovered. But in order for the group to feel safe, participants need to know it's okay *not* to share sometimes. Always invite honest disclosure, but never force someone to speak if he or she isn't comfortable doing so. (A savvy leader will follow up later with a group member who isn't comfortable sharing in a group setting to see if a one-on-one discussion is more appropriate.)

Have volunteers take turns reading excerpts from Scripture or from the commentary. The more each person is involved even in the mundane tasks, the more he or she will feel comfortable opening up in more meaningful ways.

The leader should watch the clock and keep the discussion moving. Sometimes there may be more Going Deeper questions than your group can cover in your available time. If you've had a fruitful discussion, it's okay to move on without finishing everything. And if you think the group is getting bogged down on a question or has taken off on a tangent, you can simply say, "Let's go on to question 5." Be sure to save at least ten to fifteen minutes for the Going Forward questions.

Finally, soak your group meetings in prayer—before you begin, during as needed, and always at the end of your time together.

The Prophet
(EZEKIEL 1—3)

Before you begin ...
- *Pray for the Holy Spirit to reveal truth and wisdom as you go through this lesson.*
- *Read Ezekiel 1—3. This lesson references chapter 1 in* Be Reverent. *It will be helpful for you to have your Bible and a copy of the commentary available as you work through this lesson.*

Getting Started

From the Commentary

Like Jeremiah (1:2), Zechariah (1:1), and John the Baptist (Luke 1:5ff.), Ezekiel ("God strengthens") was called by God from being a priest to serving as a prophet. As God's spokesman to the Jewish exiles in the land of Babylon, he would rebuke them for their sins and expose their idolatry, but he would also reveal the glorious future the Lord had prepared for them. He was thirty years old at the time of his call (Ezek. 1:1), the normal age for a priest to begin his ministry (Num. 4:1–3, 23).

It would have been much easier for Ezekiel to remain a priest, for priests were highly esteemed by the Jews, and a priest could read the law and learn everything he needed to know to do his work. Prophets were usually despised and persecuted. They received their messages and orders from the Lord as the occasion demanded and could never be sure what would happen next. It was dangerous to be a prophet. Most people resent being told about their sins and prefer to hear messages of cheer, not declarations of judgment.

—*Be Reverent*, page 13

1. Why did God choose a priest to become a prophet? What was unique about this change of "purpose" for Ezekiel? Why didn't he reject God's call? Why might a prophet's influence be more significant in Babylon than a priest's?

More to Consider: Jeremiah had been ministering in Jerusalem for four years when Ezekiel was born in 622 BC, and surely as he grew up, he paid attention to what Jeremiah was saying. It's also likely that Daniel and Ezekiel knew each other before the captivity, though there's no evidence they saw each other in Babylon. False prophets were giving Jewish people false hopes of quick deliverance. Jeremiah's letter told the Jews they'd be in captivity for seventy years (Jer. 29:8–10). Based on all of this, why would Ezekiel's prophetic ministry be so critical to the Jews? Why was so much prophecy in the Old Testament controversial to the people whom it targeted?

2. Choose one verse or phrase from Ezekiel 1—3 that stands out to you. This could be something you're intrigued by, something that makes you uncomfortable, something that puzzles you, something that resonates with you, or just something you want to examine further. Write that here.

Going Deeper

From the Commentary

> The kingdom of Judah had suffered greatly at the hands of victorious Babylon, and many Jewish people wondered if Jehovah was still the God of Abraham, Isaac, and Jacob

(see Ps. 74). Were the Jews not God's chosen people? Had not Jehovah defeated their enemies and given them the Promised Land? Was not Jerusalem His Holy City, and did He not dwell in their holy temple? Yet now His chosen people were exiles in a pagan land, their Promised Land was devastated, Jerusalem was in enemy hands, and the temple had been robbed of its precious treasures. It was a dark day for Israel, and the first thing Ezekiel needed to understand was that, no matter how discouraging the circumstances, God was still on the throne accomplishing His divine purposes in the world.

—*Be Reverent*, pages 14–15

3. There are many unexplained mysteries in the vision Ezekiel had, but one message comes through with clarity and power: Jehovah is the sovereign Lord of Israel and of all the nations of the earth. Why was this so important to the Jews, considering their current circumstance? What did it mean to the Jews that Jehovah was the Lord of all nations? What hope would that have given them? Why might that message also have caused them to doubt God?

From the Commentary

The word of the Lord came to Ezekiel in the form of a vision, and the hand of the Lord laid hold of him and claimed him for special service. The phrase "the word of the Lord came" is used fifty times in his prophecy and speaks of the authority of his message, and "the hand of the LORD" is found also in Ezekiel 3:14, 22; 8:1; 33:22; 37:1; and 40:1. The word of the Lord brings enlightenment and the hand of the Lord enablement (see Eph. 1:15–23). In Scripture, a storm is often an image of divine judgment (Prov. 1:27; Isa. 66:15; Jer. 4:13; 23:19; Nah. 1:3). Since the immense whirlwind cloud Ezekiel beheld was coming from the north, it indicated the invasion of Judah by the Babylonian army and the destruction of the land, the city of Jerusalem, and the temple (Jer. 4:6; 6:1). For forty years, God had graciously led Israel by a fiery cloud, but now a fiery cloud was bringing chastening to His disobedient people. The prophet Jeremiah saw a similar vision at the beginning of his ministry (Jer. 1:13–16).

Ezekiel saw bright light around the cloud and an enfolding fire, like molten metal, within the cloud. Both are reminders of the holiness of God, for "our God is a consuming fire" (Ex. 19:16, 18; Deut. 4:24; Heb. 12:29).

—*Be Reverent*, pages 15–16

4. Why did Ezekiel use the words *like* and *likeness* so often when describing the vision in chapter 1? How did God use similar images (bronze, lion, lightning, etc.) throughout the Bible to illustrate spiritual truths?

From Today's World

Prophets in the Old Testament frequently had visions like the one described in Ezekiel. And like Ezekiel's vision, they often included tons of symbolism—from the descriptions of the cherubim having four faces (man, lion, ox, and eagle) to the wheels within wheels. It was the prophet's job to interpret these images so they made sense for the people to whom they were targeted. While some modern believers claim to receive visions from God, there hasn't been a universally acclaimed prophet in the church for hundreds of years. Thus, most of our interpretive efforts as a church are focused on the events recorded in Scripture. We see the record of Ezekiel's dream and try to interpret what it means not only for the Jews in captivity but also for believers today.

5. Why are there no prophets like Ezekiel today? What are the benefits of studying the prophecies of old and what they meant for the people whom they immediately affected? What are the benefits of studying the implications for modern times? How can God reveal new truths from old prophecies?

From the Commentary

> There were four wheels in the vision (Ezek. 1:16), each with
> an intersecting wheel and each associated with one of the
> cherubim. The intersecting wheels enabled the creatures
> and the cloud to move in any direction instantly without
> having to turn, moving like a flash of lightning. These
> wheels looked like chrysolite, a yellow or greenish-yellow
> precious stone; they were very high, as though reaching
> from earth to heaven, and their rims were awesome and
> full of eyes. The spirit (Spirit) of the living creatures was in
> the wheels, so that the living creatures moved in whatever
> direction the wheels moved. It was indeed an awesome
> sight, the huge wheels, the living creatures, the enfolding
> fire, and the eyes in the rims of the wheels.
>
> —*Be Reverent*, page 17

6. Review Ezekiel 1:15–21. How was this imagery a picture of the
providence of God? In what ways did it reveal that God is always at work,
never wrong, and never late? How did this last truth (God is never late) in
particular speak to the captives in Babylon?

From the Commentary

The glory of the Lord is one of the key themes in Ezekiel (3:12, 23; 8:4; 9:3; 10:4, 18–19; 11:22–23; 39:21; 43:2, 4–5; 44:4). The prophet will watch God's glory leave the temple and go over the Mount of Olives, and he will also see it return to the kingdom temple. Because of Israel's sins, the glory left the temple, but God's promise is that one day the city of Jerusalem and the temple will be blessed by the glorious presence of the Lord. The city will be called "Jehovah Shammah—the Lord is there" (48:35).

Now we can begin to grasp the message that God was giving His prophet. Though His people were in exile and their nation was about to be destroyed, God was still on the throne and able to handle every situation. In His marvelous providence, He moves in the affairs of nations and works out His hidden plan. Israel wasn't the victim of Babylonian aggression. It was God who enabled the Babylonians to conquer His people and chasten them for their rebellion, but God would also bring the Medes and the Persians to conquer Babylon, and Cyrus, king of Persia, would permit the Jews to return to their land.

—*Be Reverent*, pages 18–19

7. Read Romans 11:33. How does this passage speak to the prophetic message that God was still on the throne, even as the Jews suffered in captivity? How does this message apply equally today? What are some of

the ways today's God-followers suffer from "captivity"? How can we see God in the midst of that?

From the Commentary

As a result of beholding the vision, Ezekiel fell to the ground, completely overwhelmed by the glory of the Lord and the wonder of His providential working in the world. Who but the sovereign Lord could have a throne like a chariot and move as quickly as He pleased? Who but the Lord could travel in the midst of a fiery whirlwind to accomplish His great purposes?

Ezekiel is called "son of man" ninety-three times in his book, a title that the Lord also gave to Daniel (Dan. 8:17). "Son of Man" is also a messianic title (Dan. 7:13), which the Lord Jesus applied to Himself at least eighty-two times when He was ministering on earth. But in the case of Daniel and Ezekiel, the title "son of man" emphasized their humanity and mortality. Ezekiel was facedown in the dust when God spoke to him, reminding him and us of humankind's humble beginning in the dust (Gen. 1:26; 3:19). "For He knows our frame; He remembers that we are dust" (Ps. 103:14 NKJV). God remembers, but sometimes we forget.

—*Be Reverent*, page 19

8. What is the symbolism of Ezekiel being facedown in the dust when God spoke to him? (See Gen. 1:26; 3:19.) Do you think this posture before God is relevant today? Why or why not? Why was Ezekiel called "son of man"? (See also Dan. 8:17.) In what ways was Jesus like Ezekiel in being a son of man? In what ways did the phrase have a different meaning when Jesus applied it to Himself?

More to Consider: Prophets weren't people who majored only in foretelling the future, although that was part of their ministry. They were primarily "forth-tellers." What is the difference between a fortune-teller and a forth-teller? What usually followed a prophet's message of judgment? Why did God tag such difficult-to-hear messages with these kinds of promises?

From the Commentary

Being a priest, Ezekiel knew that the Hebrew Scriptures pictured God's Word as food to be received within the heart and digested inwardly. Job valued God's Word more than his "necessary food" (Job 23:12), and Moses admonished the Jews to live on God's Word as well as on the bread (manna) that the Lord supplied daily (Deut. 8:3; see Matt. 4:4). The prophet Jeremiah "ate" the Word of God (Jer. 15:16), and so did the apostle John (Rev. 10:8–10). God's prophets must speak from within their hearts or their messages will not be authentic.

A hand stretched out and handed Ezekiel a scroll that didn't have any good news written on it, because it was filled on both sides with "words of lament and mourning and woe" (Ezek. 2:10 NIV). Perhaps it contained the messages that are recorded in chapters 4 through 32, God's judgments on Jerusalem and the Gentile nations. God commanded him to eat the scroll, and it tasted sweet like honey (Ps. 19:10; 119:103), although later he tasted bitterness (Ezek. 3:14), not unlike the apostle John (Rev. 10:8–11). It's a great honor to be a spokesperson for the Lord, but we must be able to handle both the bitter and the sweet.

—Be Reverent, page 21

9. Why did God instruct Ezekiel to eat the scroll? Why did it taste sweet initially (see Ps. 19:10; 119:103), then bitter later (see Rev. 10:8–11)? What

were the "sweet" and "bitter" things Ezekiel was asked to handle on behalf of the Lord? What are some of the sweet and bitter things we are asked to handle today?

From the Commentary

> What the people needed more than anything else was to hear the Word of the Lord. Even before the nation fell, Jeremiah had warned them not to listen to the false prophets, but neither the leaders nor the common people would obey (Jer. 5:30–31; 6:14; 7:8; 8:10). God had spoken loudly in Israel's shameful defeat and captivity, but now the Jews were still clinging to empty hopes and listening to the lying words of false prophets in Babylon (Jer. 29:15–32). The human heart would rather hear lies that bring comfort than truths that bring conviction and cleansing.
>
> —*Be Reverent*, page 22

10. Review Ezekiel 3:4–27. How did Ezekiel declare God's word as a messenger (3:4–10); a sufferer (vv. 10–15); a watchman (vv. 16–21); and a

sign (vv. 22–27)? How was each of these descriptions of him essential to his message? How would each have been received differently by the people? What lesson is there for us today in how God used these different images?

Looking Inward

Take a moment to reflect on all that you've explored thus far in this study of Ezekiel 1—3. Review your notes and answers and think about how each of these things matters in your life today.

> *Tips for Small Groups: To get the most out of this section, form pairs or trios and have group members take turns answering these questions. Be honest and as open as you can in this discussion, but most of all, be encouraging and supportive of others. Be sensitive to those who are going through particularly difficult times, and don't press for people to speak if they're uncomfortable doing so.*

11. How would you react today if God called you to be His prophet? What would your initial response be if God asked you to preach a message of judgment to His people? What does this reaction tell you about your own relationship with God? Your understanding of prophecy?

12. Ezekiel's visions were packed with symbolism. What are some of the symbols in your church experience that mean the most to you? What is the benefit of communicating with others through symbolic language? What are the challenges?

13. Who are some of the "watchmen" whom you look to today as you consider the dangers of the world? Why is it important to have people looking out for matters of faith? How can you be a better watchman of your own faith life?

Going Forward

14. Think of one or two things that you have learned that you'd like to work on in the coming week. Remember that this is all about quality, not quantity. It's better to work on one specific area of life and do it well than

to work on many and do poorly (or to be so overwhelmed that you simply don't try).

Do you need to go before God in a posture of humility as Ezekiel did? Be specific. Go back through Ezekiel 1—3 and put a star next to the phrase or verse that is most encouraging to you. Consider memorizing this verse.

Real-Life Application Ideas: Spend some time mentally picturing what Ezekiel saw in his vision. Let it play in your mind as a movie for at least five or ten minutes. What do you see? Hear? Think? After you spend some time soaking in the vision, make a list of some of the concerns that have been on your mind recently. Can you take your concerns before the throne and the One on the throne? How do you view your concerns in light of this vision? Are you drawn to God in this vision or pushed away? Why? Be open to what the Spirit reveals to you in this process.

Seeking Help

15. Write a prayer below (or simply pray one in silence), inviting God to work on your mind and heart in those areas you've noted in the Going Forward section. Be honest about your desires and fears.

Notes for Small Groups:

- *Look for ways to put into practice the things you wrote in the Going Forward section. Talk with other group members about your ideas and commit to being accountable to one another.*
- *During the coming week, ask the Holy Spirit to continue to reveal truth to you from what you've read and studied.*
- *Before you start the next lesson, read Ezekiel 4—11. For more in-depth lesson preparation, read chapters 2 and 3, "The Death of a Great City" and "The Glory Has Departed," in* Be Reverent.

Death of a City
(EZEKIEL 4—11)

Before you begin ...
- *Pray for the Holy Spirit to reveal truth and wisdom as you go through this lesson.*
- *Read Ezekiel 4—11. This lesson references chapters 2 and 3 in* Be Reverent. *It will be helpful for you to have your Bible and a copy of the commentary available as you work through this lesson.*

Getting Started

From the Commentary

When the sons of Asaph wanted to describe the city of Jerusalem, they wrote, "Beautiful in elevation, the joy of the whole earth, is Mount Zion on the sides of the north, the city of the great King" (Ps. 48:2 NKJV). The Babylonian Talmud says, "Of the ten measures of beauty that came down to the world, Jerusalem took nine" (*Kidushin 49b*), and, "Whoever has not seen Jerusalem in its splendor has never seen a lovely city" (*Succah 51b*). Of modern Jerusalem, Samuel Heilman wrote, "It is a place in which people actually live; it is a place that lives in them." One of the Jewish exiles in Babylon wrote: "If I forget you, O Jerusalem, let my right hand forget its skill! If I do not remember you, let my tongue cling to the roof of my mouth—if I do not exalt Jerusalem above my chief joy" (Ps. 137:5–6 NKJV). When Jewish families around the world celebrate Passover, they conclude the meal with, "Next year in Jerusalem!"

—*Be Reverent*, page 31

1. Why was the proclamation that Jerusalem would be destroyed such a terrible message for the Jews to hear? What must they have been feeling as Ezekiel presented this prophecy? Why would it have been difficult for them to believe? To accept?

More to Consider: Most of the Jewish people had become so calloused they could no longer hear God's word, so the Lord commanded Ezekiel to take a different approach. The prophet mostly stayed home and didn't take part in the everyday conversation of the people. He remained silent at all times except when he had a message to deliver from the Lord. How might this approach have actually helped get the people's attention? Ezekiel was known to preach in an unusual way (through "action" sermons). Why was such creativity necessary to reach the people? What was the advantage of his becoming something of a curiosity because of his methods? What would that have cost him?

2. Choose one verse or phrase from Ezekiel 4—11 that stands out to you. This could be something you're intrigued by, something that makes you uncomfortable, something that puzzles you, something that resonates with you, or just something you want to examine further. Write that here.

Going Deeper

From the Commentary

The "tile" referenced in Ezekiel 4:1–3 was probably an unbaked brick or a soft clay tablet, both of which were commonplace in Babylon. On it, Ezekiel drew a sketch of the city of Jerusalem, which the people would easily recognize, and then he set it on the ground and began to "play soldier" as he acted out the siege of Jerusalem. Using earth and various objects, he set up fortifications around the city so nobody could get in or get out. He built a ramp to facilitate scaling the walls, and he provided battering rams for breaking down the gates and the walls. This, of course, was what would happen at Jerusalem in 588 BC when the Babylonian army began the siege of the city.

—*Be Reverent*, page 32

3. How would the spectators have reacted when Ezekiel placed a flat iron griddle between his face and the besieged city? What did the iron griddle symbolize? How would this action sermon have caught the Jews off guard? What does Ezekiel's creativity say about how God uses people to deliver His truth?

From the Commentary

The prophet Isaiah compared the invasion of an enemy to the shaving of a man's head and beard (Isa. 7:20), so

Ezekiel used that image for his fourth "action sermon." Shaving could be a part of a purification ritual (Num. 6:5; 8:7), but the Jews had to be careful how they dressed their hair and their beards (Lev. 19:27; Deut. 14:1), and the priests had to be especially careful (Lev. 21:5–6). When Ezekiel, a priest, publicly shaved his head and his beard, the people must have been stunned; but it took extreme measures to get their attention so they would get the message. The shaving of the head and the beard would be a sign of humiliation and great sorrow and mourning, and that's the way the Lord felt about the impending destruction of Jerusalem and the holy temple.

—*Be Reverent*, page 36

4. Review Ezekiel 5. How would Ezekiel's mention of a sword to shave the head be more dramatic than if he'd spoken of what would be expected—a razor? What implications does the sword have that the razor doesn't? Why was his hair divided into three parts? What did he do with each? What did each action symbolize?

From the Commentary

> God had commanded His prophet to remain silent except
> for those times when God commanded him to preach a
> special message. In Ezekiel 6—7, there are two messages
> of judgment from the Lord. The first explains that the
> idolatry of the people had defiled the land and the temple,
> and the second describes the terrible disaster that would
> come with the arrival of the Babylonian army.
>
> —*Be Reverent*, pages 38–39

5. Review Ezekiel 6. What was Ezekiel's warning to the people? Why was
God about to punish them? In 6:14, God told Ezekiel, "Then they will
know that I am the LORD." What is the purpose of this specific phrase in
this context? (The phrase appears over sixty times in the book of Ezekiel.)

From the Commentary

> The nation of Israel was blessed with a gracious Lord to
> worship and love, a fruitful land to enjoy, and a holy law
> to obey. Their love for the Lord and their obedience to

His law would determine how much blessing He could entrust to them in the land. These were the terms of the covenant, and the Jewish people knew them well. The generation that first entered the land obeyed God's covenant, as did the succeeding generation, but the third generation provoked the Lord, broke their "marriage vows," and prostituted themselves to idols (Judg. 2:10–13). They disobeyed the law, defied their Lord, and defiled the land, and the Lord would not accept that kind of conduct. First, He punished them *in their land* by permitting seven enemy nations to occupy the land and oppress the people, as recorded in the book of Judges.

—*Be Reverent*, page 42

6. Why did the Jews keep returning to the worship of idols every time God delivered them? How was the captivity in Babylon God's response to this continued disobedience? What does this tell us about how seriously God regards His covenant and our obedience? Is our obedience as important to God as the Jews' obedience was in Ezekiel's day? What difference does this make?

From the Commentary

> The Gentile nations had their temples, priests, religious laws, and sacrifices, but only the nation of Israel had the glory of the true and living God dwelling in their midst (Rom. 9:4). When Moses dedicated the tabernacle, God's glory moved in (Ex. 40:34–35), but the sins of the people caused the glory to depart (1 Sam. 4:19–22). When Solomon dedicated the temple, once again God's glory filled the sanctuary (1 Kings 8:11), but centuries later, the prophet Ezekiel watched that glory leave the temple— and then come back again! Without the presence of the glory of the Lord, God's people are just another religious crowd, going through the motions. "If Your Presence does not go with us," said Moses to the Lord, "do not bring us up from here" (Ex. 33:15 NKJV). The people of God are identified by the presence of God.
>
> —*Be Reverent*, page 49

7. Why was the vision God gave Ezekiel such a difficult message to preach? What three tragedies did the message address? (See Ezek. 8:1–18; 9:1—10:22; and 11:1–25.) Why is it important that Ezekiel's message was the opposite of what the false prophets were teaching? How did that complicate his ability to share God's truth?

From the Commentary

Seeing dramatic visions and hearing God's voice were not everyday experiences for God's servants the prophets. As far as the record is concerned, fourteen months passed since Ezekiel was called and given his first visions. During that time he and his wife lived normal lives as Jeremiah had instructed (Jer. 29:4–9). Since the exiles in Babylon didn't have Jewish kings or princes to direct the affairs of the people, they chose elders to be their leaders, and some of these elders occasionally visited Ezekiel (see Ezek. 14:1; 20:1; 33:30–33).

—*Be Reverent*, page 50

8. What were the vivid experiences Ezekiel had in chapters 8 and 9? What was the sad conclusion that followed these experiences? What was God's response after the repeated rebellion of His people? Can this happen today? Explain.

More to Consider: The strange phrase "putting the branch to their nose" (Ezek. 8:17) has no parallel in Scripture and may describe a part of an idolatrous ritual. What was God's response to this gesture? What does that suggest about its meaning?

From the Commentary

The heart of Ezekiel's message is that the people are doomed (Ezek. 9:1—10:22), and it must have broken his heart to deliver it. Read the book of Lamentations to see how thoroughly the Lord "dealt in fury" with His people. Jeremiah was an eyewitness of the destruction of Jerusalem, and what Ezekiel predicted, Jeremiah saw fulfilled.

In all of this, Ezekiel was learning that the most important part of the nation's life was to magnify the glory of God. The presence of God in the sanctuary was a great privilege for the people of Israel, but it was also a great responsibility. The glory of God cannot dwell with the sins of God's people, so it was necessary for the glory to leave, and the sanctuary and the people to be judged.

—*Be Reverent*, pages 54–55, 58

9. What is God's glory? Why is glory such an important theme in Ezekiel's message? What does this theme tell us about God's people during this time in history? What were some of the ways they were being irreverent? What are similar challenges in the church today?

From the Commentary

Ezekiel was still having his vision of Jerusalem and the temple, and the Lord showed him twenty-five men at the eastern door of the temple, worshipping the sun. (See Ezek. 8:15–18.) Among them were the leaders of the people, Jaazaniah and Pelatiah. (This is not the Jaazaniah of 8:11.) These men were giving wicked advice to the king and other leaders in Jerusalem, but their counsel was not from the Lord. How could it be wise counsel when they were idolaters who worshipped the sun? At the same time, they were plotting evil so that they could benefit personally from the Babylonian attack on the city. In every crisis, you will find "opportunists" who seek to help themselves instead of helping their country, and they usually hide behind the mask of patriotism.

Not only were these leaders idolaters and wicked counselors, but they cultivated a philosophy that gave them and the other leaders a false confidence in their dangerous situation. "Is not the time near to build houses?" they asked. "This city is the pot and we are the flesh" (Ezek. 11:3 NASB). Jeremiah had told the exiles to build houses in Babylon and settle down and raise families, because they would live there for seventy years (Jer. 29:4ff.). But it was foolish for the people in Jerusalem to build houses, for the Lord had ordained that the Babylonian army would destroy the city and slaughter most of the inhabitants. These evil leaders were sure that Jerusalem was as safe for them as a piece of meat in a cooking pot. The innuendo in this metaphor was that the people in Jerusalem were choice cuts of meat, while the exiles in Babylon were just the scraps and rejected pieces. Of course, just the opposite was true! Had the leaders in Jerusalem listened to Jeremiah's message about the baskets of figs, they would have seen their philosophy completely reversed. The good figs were the exiles and the bad figs were the people left in Jerusalem (Jer. 24:1–7). God would preserve a remnant from among the exiles, but the idolaters in Jerusalem would be slain.

The Lord told Ezekiel to prophesy against those evil leaders and point out that they weren't the meat—they were the butchers! They had killed innocent people in Jerusalem and stolen their possessions, and even if the leaders weren't slain in Jerusalem, they would not escape judgment. They might flee the city, but the Babylonians would catch them at the border, pass sentence on them, and kill them; and that is exactly what happened (2 Kings 25:18–21; Jer. 39:1–7; 52:1–11, 24–27). Then the Jewish officials would learn too late that Jehovah alone is Lord of heaven and earth.

—*Be Reverent*, pages 59–60

10. Review Ezekiel 11:1–13. What happened when Ezekiel preached his message in this passage? How was this vivid proof to the sun worshippers that their plans would lead to disaster? How did Ezekiel reveal his shepherd's heart at the end of his vision? What was his request of the Lord?

Looking Inward

Take a moment to reflect on all that you've explored thus far in this study of Ezekiel 4—11. Review your notes and answers and think about how each of these things matters in your life today.

> *Tips for Small Groups:* To get the most out of this section, form pairs or trios and have group members take turns answering these questions. Be honest and as open as you can in this discussion, but most of all, be encouraging and supportive of others. Be sensitive to those who are going through particularly difficult times, and don't press for people to speak if they're uncomfortable doing so.

11. Ezekiel used creative methods to deliver some of his sermons. What are some of the most memorable sermons you've experienced? What made them memorable?

12. What are some of the idols that tempt you away from God? How do you prepare yourself for dealing with those temptations? When you do stray, what brings you back to God?

13. What are some ways you struggle to show reverence to God? What does reverence mean to you? What does it look like in your life?

Going Forward

14. Think of one or two things that you have learned that you'd like to work on in the coming week. Remember that this is all about quality, not quantity. It's better to work on one specific area of life and do it well than to work on many and do poorly (or to be so overwhelmed that you simply don't try).

Do you want to address an idol in your life? Be specific. Go back through Ezekiel 4—11 and put a star next to the phrase or verse that is most encouraging to you. Consider memorizing this verse.

Real-Life Application Ideas: Ezekiel's creative message delivery would have captured the people's attention. Whether they chose to obey what God was telling them was another story. But the creativity is notable. This week, come up with a creative way to deliver a specific message to family members, friends, or even your small group. It doesn't have to be anything big. Just choose a message—something God has been helping you with lately—and then brainstorm a creative method for teaching that using symbolism or interactivity or role-playing. Whatever you like. After you've shared the message, talk with your participants or audience about the experience. What did you learn in the process of teaching? What does this suggest about the way God's message is shared? Use what you learn in your life as you interact with seekers and others who have an interest in matters of the faith.

Seeking Help

15. Write a prayer below (or simply pray one in silence), inviting God to work on your mind and heart in those areas you've noted in the Going Forward section. Be honest about your desires and fears.

Notes for Small Groups:

- *Look for ways to put into practice the things you wrote in the Going Forward section. Talk with other group members about your ideas and commit to being accountable to one another.*

- *During the coming week, ask the Holy Spirit to continue to reveal truth to you from what you've read and studied.*

- *Before you start the next lesson, read Ezekiel 12—17. For more in-depth lesson preparation, read chapters 4 and 5, "The Truth about the False" and "Pictures of Failure," in* Be Reverent.

Failure
(EZEKIEL 12—17)

Before you begin ...
- *Pray for the Holy Spirit to reveal truth and wisdom as you go through this lesson.*
- *Read Ezekiel 12—17. This lesson references chapters 4 and 5 in* Be Reverent. *It will be helpful for you to have your Bible and a copy of the commentary available as you work through this lesson.*

Getting Started

From the Commentary

In his *Notes on the State of Virginia*, Thomas Jefferson wrote, "It is error alone which needs the support of government. Truth can stand by itself." During the siege of Jerusalem (606–586 BC), error had the support of government and religious leaders, and most of the Jewish exiles in Babylon agreed with them. "We will never give in to the Babylonian army!" was the cry of the Jewish people in Jerusalem. "The Lord will never allow the Gentiles to destroy His Holy City or defile His holy temple!" One dissenting voice in Jerusalem was Jeremiah; in Babylon it was Ezekiel. Both in his "action sermons" and his oral messages, Ezekiel warned the people that they were trusting in illusions.

—*Be Reverent*, page 67

1. What were the illusions that the people trusted in when they should have been trusting in God? Why did they resist the message that the city and nation were doomed? How did Ezekiel expose the errors that led to the ruin?

2. Choose one verse or phrase from Ezekiel 12—17 that stands out to you. This could be something you're intrigued by, something that makes you uncomfortable, something that puzzles you, something that resonates with you, or just something you want to examine further. Write that here.

Going Deeper

From the Commentary

> When the Lord called Ezekiel, He warned him that he
> would be ministering to a rebellious people (Ezek. 2:3–8)
> who were spiritually blind and deaf (12:2). In order to
> understand God's truth, we must be obedient to God's
> will (John 7:17; Ps. 25:8–10), but Israel was far from
> being obedient. Years before, Isaiah spoke to people who
> were spiritually blind and deaf (Isa. 6:9–10), and those
> were the kind of people Jeremiah was preaching to in
> Jerusalem (Jer. 5:21). When our Lord was here on earth,
> many of the people were spiritually blind and deaf (Matt.
> 13:13–14), and so were the people who heard Paul (Acts
> 28:26–28).
>
> —*Be Reverent*, pages 67–68

3. How did Ezekiel get the attention of the exiles and excite their interest
in 12:1–16? In 12:17–28? Why were the people hesitant to believe Ezekiel's
message? What did they say in response to the message (12:22)?

More to Consider: Read Isaiah 5:19. In what ways were the Jews here saying something similar to the Jews who rejected Ezekiel's message about the impending doom? How do people have the same attitude today about Jesus' return? (See 2 Peter 3.)

From the Commentary

Ezekiel had answered the shallow, selfish thinking of the exiles and the people in Jerusalem, but now he attacked the source of their blind optimism: the messages of the false prophets. Jeremiah in Jerusalem had to confront a similar group of men who claimed to have a word from the Lord. The false prophets claimed to speak in the name of the Lord, just as Jeremiah and Ezekiel did, but they didn't get their messages from the Lord. Ezekiel spoke against both false prophets (Ezek. 13:1–16) and false prophetesses (vv. 17–23) who were actually using the occult practices forbidden to the people of Israel (Deut. 18:9–14).

—*Be Reverent*, page 71

4. Review Ezekiel 13. What did Ezekiel say about the false prophets? About their false prophecies? Why was the method by which they were getting their "prophecies" an issue? Is this something that the church deals with today? Explain.

From the Commentary

God explained how He would judge the false prophets (Ezek. 13:9). They would be exposed as counterfeits and no longer have an exalted reputation among the people. They would lose their prominent places in the councils of the nation. God would treat them like Jews who had also lost their citizenship (Ezra 2:59, 62) and were therefore deprived of the privilege of returning to their land. It appears that the false prophets in Jerusalem would be slain by the enemy, and those in Babylon would be left there to die. The counterfeit prophets gave the people a false hope, so God gave them no hope at all.

It's a serious thing to be called of God and to speak His Word to His people. To assume a place of ministry without being called and gifted is arrogance, and to manufacture messages without receiving them from the Lord is impertinence. The false prophets in Ezekiel's day were guilty of both. Popularity is not a test of truth.

—*Be Reverent*, pages 72–73

5. Respond to this statement in light of what Ezekiel was facing: Popularity is not a test of truth. Why were the false prophets so popular? How is this a problem even today? Why does popularity continue to drive people to false truth?

From the Commentary

> Except when God told him to leave, Ezekiel was confined
> to his house (Ezek. 3:24) and was not allowed to speak
> unless he was declaring a message from the Lord. The
> elders of the exiled people came to visit him to see what
> he was doing and to hear what he had to say about their
> situation (8:1; 20:1). The prophet gave them two messages
> from the Lord.
>
> (1) He exposed their hidden sin (Ezek. 14:1–5).
>
> (2) He called them to repent (Ezek. 14:6–11).
>
> —*Be Reverent*, pages 74–75

6. What does the manner in which God used Ezekiel reveal about God's
approach to the Jews in captivity? Why did Ezekiel remain confined to
his house most of the time? Is there a message for the church today in this
story? If so, what is it? The message Ezekiel gave to those who visited him
sounds like a broken record. Why did the people keep coming back if all
they ever heard was, "You're sinning; repent"?

From the Commentary

The prophet Ezekiel remained silent except when the word of the Lord came to him and God permitted him to speak (Ezek. 3:25–27). The three messages recorded in Ezekiel 15—17 were given to the elders who were seated before him in his own house, men who outwardly appeared interested in hearing God's word but inwardly were idolatrous (14:1–3). The Lord knew that neither the elders nor the people took Ezekiel's messages seriously because they saw him as a religious entertainer whose words were only beautiful music (33:30–33). Whenever God's people turn from His Word and become satisfied with substitutes, they are indeed headed for failure.

Because the people who heard him were spiritually blind and deaf, Ezekiel had to hold their attention, arouse their interest, and motivate them to think about God's truth. One way he did this was through his "action sermons," and another way was by means of sermons filled with vivid and arresting vocabulary and intriguing imagery. In the three messages in chapters 15—17, Ezekiel spoke about a vine, an unfaithful wife, and three shoots from a tree, and each of these images conveyed God's truth to those who really wanted to understand.

—*Be Reverent*, page 83

7. Describe some of the vivid language and teaching methods Ezekiel used in chapters 15—17. What was the point of each of these three pictures and parables? What judgments did they proclaim?

From the Commentary

> The vine is an image found frequently in Scripture. Jesus compared Himself to a vine and His disciples to branches in the vine, because we depend wholly on Him for life and fruitfulness (John 15). Without Him, we can do nothing. Revelation 14:17–20 speaks of "the vine of the earth," a symbol of corrupt Gentile society at the end of the age, ripening for judgment in the winepress of God's wrath. But the image of the vine is often applied to the nation of Israel (Ps. 80; Isa. 5:1–7; Jer. 2:21; Matt. 21:28–46; Luke 20:9–19). In fact, Ezekiel will bring the image of the vine into his parable about the "shoots" (Ezek. 17:6–8 NIV).
>
> —*Be Reverent*, page 84

8. Review Ezekiel 15. What does this chapter tell us about Israel's status when God planted her in the Promised Land? About how she increased and prospered? Why is the vine imagery so perfect for this message?

From the Commentary

Ezekiel 16 contains some of the most vivid language found anywhere in Scripture. It is addressed to the city of Jerusalem but refers to the entire nation. The chapter traces the spiritual history of the Jews from "birth" (God's call of Abraham) through "marriage" (God's covenant with the people), and up to their "spiritual prostitution" (idolatry) and the sad consequences that followed (ruin and exile). The Lord takes His "wife" to court and bears witness of her unfaithfulness to Him. At the same time, the Lord is replying to the complaints of the people that He had not kept His promises when He allowed the Babylonians to invade the land. God did keep His covenant; it was Israel who broke her marriage vow and also broke the heart of her Lord and invited His chastening (Ezek. 6:9).

—*Be Reverent*, page 86

9. Review Ezekiel 16. How does this illustration reveal the dark side of Israel's wickedness? How does it also reveal the light of God's grace? (See also Rom. 5:20.)

More to Consider: When Israel became prosperous and famous, she forgot the Lord who gave her such great wealth, and she began to use God's generous gifts for worshipping idols. (See Deut. 6:10–12; 8:10–20; Hosea 2:8, 13–14.) How did this play out in the Israelites' daily lives? In what ways did they begin to worship the creation rather than the Creator? (See Rom. 1:21–25.) How does this reflect the behavior of some of us today?

From the Commentary

From the images of a vine and a marriage, Ezekiel turned to the image of a great tree, two eagles, and three shoots. This message is called a parable or riddle, which means a story with a deeper meaning, an allegory in which various objects refer to people and what they do. The Jewish people were fond of discussing the wise sayings of the ancients and were always seeking to discover deeper meanings (Ps. 78:1–3).

—*Be Reverent,* page 93

10. Review Ezekiel 17. What was the purpose of this allegory? Who were the three shoots? The eagles? Why did Ezekiel deliver this message in allegorical or proverbial form? How is this similar to the way Jesus often taught His disciples? What are the benefits of teaching through parable or allegory?

Looking Inward

Take a moment to reflect on all that you've explored thus far in this study of Ezekiel 12—17. Review your notes and answers and think about how each of these things matters in your life today.

Tips for Small Groups: To get the most out of this section, form pairs or trios and have group members take turns answering these questions. Be honest and as open as you can in this discussion, but most of all, be encouraging and supportive of others. Be sensitive to those who are going through particularly difficult times, and don't press for people to speak if they're uncomfortable doing so.

11. Ezekiel had a difficult job because the false prophets were preaching a much more welcome message. The people wanted to hear good news, not doom and gloom. Have you ever accepted or agreed with a teaching or prophecy because it supported what you wanted to believe, not what was actually true? What role does trusting God play in how you sort through questionable teachings?

12. Have you ever fallen for a false prophecy or belief because of someone's popularity? Explain. What is an example of a truth that wasn't popular that you embraced? What does this tension tell you about the cost of following Christ?

13. Describe a time when someone taught you an important message through a story or parable. How did that experience differ from straight-ahead preaching or teaching methods? Why did it resonate with you? What did it reveal to you about the way in which you most effectively learn?

Going Forward

14. Think of one or two things that you have learned that you'd like to work on in the coming week. Remember that this is all about quality, not quantity. It's better to work on one specific area of life and do it well than to work on many and do poorly (or to be so overwhelmed that you simply don't try).

Do you want to learn how to trust God's wisdom even when it's not always what you want to hear? Be specific. Go back through Ezekiel

12—17 and put a star next to the phrase or verse that is most encouraging to you. Consider memorizing this verse.

> *Real-Life Application Ideas: The message in these chapters is ultimately about God's promises for His people. Even though His people were in a dark period in their history, God was not absent. This week, spend some time looking at the darkest places in your life—the struggles and the challenges, the losses and the disappointments. But don't just stay in those places; look around and see that God is still there, still shining His light of truth and grace. Take some time to thank God for His never-ending presence. Then work on seeing that light and grace as you encounter those difficult times from now on.*

Seeking Help

15. Write a prayer below (or simply pray one in silence), inviting God to work on your mind and heart in those areas you've noted in the Going Forward section. Be honest about your desires and fears.

Notes for Small Groups:

- *Look for ways to put into practice the things you wrote in the Going Forward section. Talk with other group members about your ideas and commit to being accountable to one another.*

- *During the coming week, ask the Holy Spirit to continue to reveal truth to you from what you've read and studied.*

- *Before you start the next lesson, read Ezekiel 18—21. For more in-depth lesson preparation, read chapter 6, "God Is Just!," in* Be Reverent.

A Just God
(EZEKIEL 18—21)

Before you begin ...
- *Pray for the Holy Spirit to reveal truth and wisdom as you go through this lesson.*
- *Read Ezekiel 18—21. This lesson references chapter 6 in* Be Reverent. *It will be helpful for you to have your Bible and a copy of the commentary available as you work through this lesson.*

Getting Started

From the Commentary

Responsibility is one of the major themes of these four chapters. The Jewish exiles in Babylon were blaming their ancestors for the terrible judgment that had befallen them, so Ezekiel explained that God judges people individually for their own sins and not for somebody else's sins (Ezek. 18). He then pointed out that the Jewish leaders were responsible for the foolish decisions they had made (Ezek. 19), and that the nation itself had a long history of irresponsibility (Ezek. 20). Finally, the prophet reminded his listeners that the Lord Jehovah also had a responsibility to be faithful to Himself and His covenant with the Jews, and this was why He had chastened them (Ezek. 21).

—*Be Reverent*, page 99

1. How was Ezekiel able to answer the people's complaints that the Lord was treating them unfairly? Why is responsibility such an important theme in Ezekiel's message? Why is it so important for the church today?

More to Consider: In his Devil's Dictionary, *the cynical Ambrose Bierce defined responsibility as "a detachable burden easily shifted to the shoulders of God, Fate, Fortune, luck, or one's neighbor." What are some examples of this kind of "shifting" as recorded in the Bible? (For example, see the story of Adam and Eve.) What does it mean that "privilege always brings responsibility"?*

2. Choose one verse or phrase from Ezekiel 18—21 that stands out to you. This could be something you're intrigued by, something that makes you

uncomfortable, something that puzzles you, something that resonates with you, or just something you want to examine further. Write that here.

Going Deeper

From the Commentary

As you read Ezekiel 18, you find the prophet answering the erroneous statements the Jewish exiles were making about God and their difficult situation (vv. 2, 19, 25, 29). God knew what His people were saying and so did His prophet. Ignoring the inspired Word of God, the people were building their case on a popular proverb: "The fathers have eaten sour grapes, and the children's teeth are set on edge." In other words, "Our fathers have sinned and we, their children, are being punished for it." Their philosophy was a kind of irresponsible fatalism. "No matter what we do," they argued, "we still have to suffer because of what the older generation did." The prophet Jeremiah quoted the same familiar proverb and preached the same truth that Ezekiel preached: God deals with us as individuals and punishes each of us justly for what we do (Jer. 31:29–30). He is a just and righteous God who shows no partiality (Deut. 10:17; 32:4). If He withholds punishment, it's only because of His grace and merciful longsuffering.

—*Be Reverent*, page 100

3. Where did Ezekiel's audience get the idea that God punished the children for their fathers' sins? (See for example: Exod. 20:5; 34:6–7; Num. 14:18; Deut. 7:9–10.) Why was this a misreading of Scripture? How did this go against what Moses had taught? (See Deut. 24:16.) How did Ezekiel answer the people's objections?

From the Commentary

The prophet refutes the proverb by imagining a situation involving three men in a family, people with whom his listeners certainly could identify. He began with *a righteous father* (Ezek. 18:5–9), a hypothetical Jew who kept God's law and therefore was just and would not die because of sin (vv. 4, 9). Death is frequently mentioned in this chapter (vv. 4, 13, 17–18, 20–21, 23–24, 26, 28, 32) and refers to physical death and not necessarily eternal punishment, although any Jew who didn't exercise saving faith in the Lord would not be accepted by Him. Whether people lived under the old covenant or the new covenant, before or since the cross, the way of salvation is the same: faith in the Lord that is evidenced by a new life of obedience (Heb. 11:6; Hab. 2:4; see Rom. 4).

—*Be Reverent*, page 101

4. Review Ezekiel 18:5–18. What were the eight negative offenses Ezekiel used to describe the man in this hypothetical situation? What were the eight positive virtues? How does this story refute the popular proverb the people were accepting as truth? ("The fathers have eaten sour grapes, and the children's teeth are set on edge.")

From Today's World

Blame has become one of the most popular "games" in modern society. You don't have to look very far to find someone blaming someone else for a circumstance or result. Of course it's hugely popular in politics, but you'll find the blame game being played equally often and well in families, workplaces, and churches. It seems so much easier to blame someone else than to own up to our own choices and the consequences of those choices.

Blame is so popular that Hollywood has made an industry of it with all the television shows featuring two parties battling it out in a courtroom setting. While there's certainly a lot to be said for due process, these shows are more about watching two people arm wrestle over who gets the most blame.

5. Why is the blame game so popular in our society today? Why aren't people owning up to their decisions and actions? What is the godly way to deal with responsibility at home? At the workplace? In society at large? How might our world look different if people were quick to take responsibility for their words and actions?

From the Commentary

In Ezekiel 18:19–24, Ezekiel responded to the questions of his hearers given in verse 19, just as he had responded to their question in verse 2. He described a wicked man who repented, turned from his sins, and lived (vv. 19–23), and then described a righteous man who returned to his sins and died (v. 24). The lesson from these two examples is obvious and answered their questions: *People determine their own character and destiny by the decisions that they make*. Neither the exiles in Babylon nor the citizens in Jerusalem were the prisoners and victims of some cosmic determinism that forced them to act as they did. Their own unbelief (they rejected Jeremiah's message) and disobedience (they worshipped heathen idols and defiled the temple) brought the Babylonian army to their gates; and Zedekiah's breaking of the covenant with Nebuchadnezzar brought the army back to destroy Jerusalem.

—*Be Reverent*, page 103

6. In what ways was this message a message of hope? What was God's promise to His people if they truly repented and turned to the Lord? (See 1 Kings 8:46–53; Jer. 29:10–14.)

From the Commentary

In Ezekiel 18:25–32, Ezekiel quoted the words of the complaining exiles for the third time: "The way of the LORD is not equal" (v. 25, see vv. 2, 19). The word *equal* means "fair." They were saying that God wasn't "playing fair" with His people. But Ezekiel pointed out that it was the people who weren't being fair with God! When they obeyed the Lord, they wanted Him to keep the terms of the covenant that promised blessing, but when they disobeyed, they didn't want Him to keep the terms of the covenant that brought chastening. They wanted God to act contrary to His own Word and His own holy nature.

"God is light" (1 John 1:5), which means He is holy and just, and "God is love" (4:8, 16), and His love is a holy love. Nowhere does Scripture say that we're saved from our sins by God's love, because salvation is by the grace of God (Eph. 2:8–10); and grace is love that pays a price. In His great love, God gave a gracious covenant to Israel, requiring only that they worship and serve Him alone with all their hearts. When sinners repented and sought the Lord, in His grace the Lord would forgive them; but when people deliberately rebelled against Him, in His holiness, God would punish them after bearing with them in His longsuffering.

—*Be Reverent*, pages 104–5

7. Why was fairness such a big concern to the people of Ezekiel's time? In what ways did they think they were being treated unfairly? What would being treated fairly really have meant to the people who had abandoned God? How was God's approach better than the people's interpretation of fairness?

From the Commentary

Ezekiel had made it clear that individual Jews were responsible for their own sins, but it was also true that their leaders had led them astray because they had rebelled against God. Jeremiah had told the kings of Judah to surrender to Nebuchadnezzar because he was God's chosen servant to chasten Israel, but they had refused to obey. Zedekiah, Judah's last king, had agreed to a treaty with Nebuchadnezzar but then had broken it and sought help from Egypt. It was this foolish act that moved Nebuchadnezzar to send his army to Jerusalem and destroy the city and the temple.

Whether you read secular or sacred history, you soon discover that people become like their leaders. The same people who applauded Solomon when he built the temple also applauded Jeroboam when he set up the golden calves and instituted a new religion. One of the hardest tasks of Christian leaders today is to keep our churches true to the Word of God so that people don't follow every religious celebrity whose ideas run contrary to Scripture. It appears that being popular and being "successful" are more important today than being faithful.

In discussing the sins of the leaders, Ezekiel used two familiar images—the lion (Ezek. 19:1–9) and the vine (vv. 10–14)—and he couched his message in the form of a funeral dirge for "the princes of Israel." David's exalted dynasty had come to an end, but the men holding the scepter were nothing like David. Ezekiel wouldn't even call them "kings" but instead referred to them as "princes" (v. 1; see 7:27; 12:10, 12). Instead of lamenting their demise, the funeral dirge actually ridiculed the rulers of Israel, but later (21:27) Ezekiel would announce the coming of Messiah, the Son of David, who would be a worthy king.

—*Be Reverent,* pages 105–6

8. Review Ezekiel 19. What sins of the leaders did Ezekiel address? How are these like or unlike the sins some of today's leaders commit? Why is it difficult to remain faithful to God's Word when a leader attains celebrity status? What is it about being a celebrity that changes a person? What are some good ways a popular leader can prevent the celebrity status from changing him or her?

From the Commentary

Ezekiel delivered the message in Ezekiel 20 on August 14, 591 BC, to some of the Jewish elders who came to his house to "inquire of the Lord." But the prophet knew that their hearts were not right with God and that they had no right to ask the Lord for instruction (vv. 30–32; see 14:1–3; 33:30–33). A willingness to submit and obey is the mark of the person who can seek God's guidance and expect to receive it. Ezekiel's response to their request was to review the history of the nation of Israel and point out the repeated rebellion of the people and the gracious longsuffering of the Lord.

The American editor and writer Norman Cousins wrote in a *Saturday Review* editorial (April 15, 1978), "History is a vast early warning system." But some anonymous thinker has said, "The one thing we learn from history is that we don't learn from history," or in the words of Dr. Laurence J. Peter, "History teaches us the mistakes we are going to make."

—*Be Reverent*, pages 107–8

9. How does the quote from Cousins, "History is a vast early warning system," apply to the Jews' situation? In what ways did they fail to learn from history? The Jewish historians, prophets, and psalmists wrote down the sins of the nation so people wouldn't forget. Why wasn't this enough to prevent them from making the same mistakes again? What does this say about human nature? About God's persistent love for His people despite their repeatedly bad choices?

More to Consider: Scripture teaches that God is working out His plan for the nations (see Dan. 5:21; 7:27; Acts 14:14–18; 17:22–31) and that His people Israel are at the heart of that plan. Why did God's people seem to be attempting to foil that plan? How did God use the people's repeated failures to enact His plan anyway? What does this tell us about today's church and its many weaknesses and sins? How will God use that for His purposes?

From the Commentary

In the Hebrew Scriptures, Ezekiel 21 begins with 20:45, and this is the best arrangement, for 20:45–49 introduces the coming judgment on Judah and Jerusalem. Ezekiel has explained the individual responsibility of the people and their leaders and the national responsibility of Israel. Now he focuses on the fact that God has a responsibility to punish His people when they rebel against Him.

—*Be Reverent*, page 114

10. Why was it important that Ezekiel include a mention of God's responsibility? What is God's responsibility to His people? What did it look like for God to be true to His character and His covenant when it came to the people of Ezekiel's time? What does God's responsibility to His people look like today?

Looking Inward

Take a moment to reflect on all that you've explored thus far in this study of Ezekiel 18—21. Review your notes and answers and think about how each of these things matters in your life today.

> *Tips for Small Groups: To get the most out of this section, form pairs or trios and have group members take turns answering these questions. Be honest and as open as you can in this discussion, but most of all, be encouraging and supportive of others. Be sensitive to those who are going through particularly difficult times, and don't press for people to speak if they're uncomfortable doing so.*

11. The blame game is surprisingly popular among church people. Describe a time when you were quick to attach blame for something you might have been responsible for. Why are you tempted to blame others for your mistakes or wrongs? How does it feel to blame others? What does it take for you to own up to your responsibility? How can you find that humility in life?

12. Think of a time when you felt God wasn't treating you fairly. What were the circumstances surrounding that season of life? What would

"fair" have looked like to you then? What did you learn in the process of that situation? How did God reveal more of Himself to you through that challenging time? What did you learn about fairness?

13. What is God's responsibility to you? How is that different from your expectations of God? What does it mean to you that God is just? How does that justice reveal itself in your faith life?

Going Forward

14. Think of one or two things that you have learned that you'd like to work on in the coming week. Remember that this is all about quality, not quantity. It's better to work on one specific area of life and do it well than to work on many and do poorly (or to be so overwhelmed that you simply don't try).

Do you want to learn how to be more responsible in your faith? Be specific. Go back through Ezekiel 18—21 and put a star next to the phrase or verse that is most encouraging to you. Consider memorizing this verse.

Real-Life Application Ideas: God's justice is a big theme in these chapters in Ezekiel. Think about God's justness in the world today. Are there places where you think people aren't being treated justly? What is your role in upholding God's justice? While we're not called to judge the world (that's God's job), we are called to be people of grace. Think of practical ways in which you can show that grace to people who are being treated unfairly in the world. This might mean people in your own community or people across the ocean. Then put those ideas into practice.

Seeking Help

15. Write a prayer below (or simply pray one in silence), inviting God to work on your mind and heart in those areas you've noted in the Going Forward section. Be honest about your desires and fears.

Notes for Small Groups:

- *Look for ways to put into practice the things you wrote in the Going Forward section. Talk with other group members about your ideas and commit to being accountable to one another.*

- *During the coming week, ask the Holy Spirit to continue to reveal truth to you from what you've read and studied.*

- *Before you start the next lesson, read Ezekiel 22—28. For more in-depth lesson preparation, read chapters 7 and 8, "See the Sinful City!" and "God Judges the Nations," in* Be Reverent.

Judging Nations
(EZEKIEL 22—28)

Before you begin ...
- *Pray for the Holy Spirit to reveal truth and wisdom as you go through this lesson.*
- *Read Ezekiel 22—28. This lesson references chapters 7 and 8 in* Be Reverent. *It will be helpful for you to have your Bible and a copy of the commentary available as you work through this lesson.*

Getting Started

From the Commentary

"David took the stronghold of Zion" (2 Sam. 5:7) and made Jerusalem his capital. Not only was the royal throne there but also the holy altar, for it was in Zion that God put His sanctuary. "For the LORD has chosen Zion; He has desired it for His habitation" (Ps. 132:13 NKJV). The Jews were proud of Mount Zion (Ps. 48) and claimed that the Lord loved Zion more than any other place (Ps. 87). But now the city of Jerusalem and the temple would be invaded by "unclean Gentiles" *who were brought there by the Lord!* Why would the Lord destroy His own beloved city and temple? Because His people had sinned and broken the covenant, and they were beyond remedy. Ezekiel described the true character of the "beautiful city" and named some of the sins that the people in Jerusalem were committing even while he spoke. Ezekiel had exposed the past sins of the nation, but now he brought Jerusalem into the courtroom and brought the record up-to-date.

—*Be Reverent*, pages 121–22

1. How did Ezekiel bring the record of the nation's sins "up-to-date" in chapter 22? Why was it important to show this to the people? Why might they have been resistant to seeing these truths about themselves? Why is it so difficult for people to accept the harder truths about themselves?

More to Consider: The words blood *or* bloodshed *are repeated seven times in Ezekiel 22:1–13 and speak of death and defilement. The prophet named two grievous sins: the shedding of innocent blood (injustice) and the worship of foreign gods (see Ezek. 7:23; 9:9). Why were these two sins singled out? How do both of these reflect the abuse of power? What are some examples of the same sins occurring in our world today?*

2. Choose one verse or phrase from Ezekiel 22—28 that stands out to you. This could be something you're intrigued by, something that makes you uncomfortable, something that puzzles you, something that resonates with you, or just something you want to examine further. Write that here.

Going Deeper

From the Commentary

In Ezekiel 22:9b–11, God targeted the immorality of the Jewish people, starting with their participation in the unspeakably filthy "worship" at the pagan shrines. The tragedy is that these idolatrous men brought their immorality home with them! Sons had intercourse with their own mothers or stepmothers, fathers with daughters-in-law, and brothers with sisters or half sisters! (See Lev. 18:6ff.; 20:10ff.) Men were committing adultery with a neighbor's wife or with women having their monthly period (Ezek. 18:6; Lev. 18:19; 20:18).

—*Be Reverent*, page 124

3. How is today's world similar to the circumstances described in this passage? Respond to this quote from Ruth Bell Graham: "If God doesn't judge America, He will have to apologize to Sodom and Gomorrah." In what ways are we living in a world not so dissimilar from the one Ezekiel spoke to? How is it different? What lessons can we learn from Ezekiel's message that can help us move toward God rather than away from Him?

From the Commentary

In Ezekiel 22:13–22, God strikes His hands in angry response to the sins of His people (Ezek. 6:11; 21:14, 17), and He announces that a day of reckoning is coming. The people of Jerusalem had the resolution to persist in their sins, in spite of God's warnings, but would they have the will and courage to endure God's day of judgment? His first act of judgment would be *dispersion* (22:13–16); the people would be exiled to Babylon and others scattered to the surrounding nations (vv. 15–16), some of which had already occurred. The people should have known this judgment was coming, because in His covenant, God had promised this kind of judgment (Lev. 26:27–39; Deut. 28:64–68). The Jewish people wanted to worship the gods of the Gentiles, so why not live with the Gentiles and learn how to do it? God would humiliate His people before the eyes of the Gentiles and through this experience bring His people back to Himself.

The second judgment would be *fire* (Ezek. 22:17–22), the destruction of their beloved city and temple. The prophet pictured a smelting furnace with different kinds of metals in it, and the dross (slag) being removed. That dross represented the people of Jerusalem who thought they were "the best" because they hadn't gone into exile. The image of the furnace is a familiar one in Scripture. Israel's suffering in Egypt was a furnace experience that helped to form the nation and prepare them for the exodus (Deut. 4:20; 1 Kings 8:51; Jer. 11:4). But now, God's furnace was Jerusalem, and the fire would be divine judgment for the sins of the people (Isa. 1:21–26; 31:9; Jer. 6:27–30).

—Be Reverent, pages 125–26

4. What is the significance of the two key words "melt" and "gather" in Ezekiel 22:19–22? Why had the people gathered in Jerusalem? What was God's reason for gathering them there? (See also Ezek. 24:1–14.)

From the Commentary

Ezekiel 23 is a good deal like Ezekiel 16 in that it depicts the history of the nation of Israel and its apostasy from the Lord. In both chapters, the image is that of prostitution, the nation breaking her "marriage vows" and like a harlot, turning to others for help. However, in chapter 16, the sin is idolatry, trusting the false gods of the pagans, while in chapter 23, the sin is trusting other nations to protect her. In this chapter you will find both Israel (the northern kingdom) and Judah (the southern kingdom) playing the harlot and looking for help from Assyria, Babylon, and Egypt, instead of trusting Jehovah God to guide them and rescue them.

—*Be Reverent*, pages 127–28

5. Why was it a sin for the people to trust other nations for protection? Why didn't they choose to trust God for rescue instead? How is this like (or unlike) the way today's churches sometimes trust worldly resources rather than God to do the church's work? Describe some examples of this. How can we be sure we're following God's plan in all that we do as God's church?

From the Commentary

In Ezekiel 24, God called Judah a "rebellious house" not only because they broke His laws and violated His covenant, but also because Zedekiah had broken his treaty with Babylon and incited the displeasure of Nebuchadnezzar. The image of the cooking pot takes us back to Ezekiel 11:1–13, where the Jewish leaders boasted that the Jews left in Jerusalem were better than the Jews taken off to Babylon. The Jerusalem Jews were the best "cuts of meat," while the Jews in Babylon were only the scraps! Of course, God contradicted that idea and made it clear that the exiles in Babylon would form a remnant with which He could rebuild the nation and the temple. Jeremiah had written to the exiles and instructed them to settle down, build houses, and raise families so that the remnant could continue the ministry for which the Lord had chosen Israel. God warned the Jewish leaders in Jerusalem that they weren't the meat—they were the butchers! They were guilty of shedding innocent blood, and God would judge them for their sins. If they weren't cooked in the cauldron of Jerusalem, they would eventually be slain by the swords of the Babylonian soldiers. Even if they escaped the city, they would be caught and killed.

In his parable about the cooking pot, Ezekiel used the image and vocabulary of the Jerusalem leaders. Yes, God would put "the best cuts of meat" into His pot (Jerusalem) and boil the meat and the bones (the Babylonian siege).

He wouldn't "cook" the flesh; He would consume it (Ezek. 24:10)! Then He would pour out the burned mess and *burn the pot itself!* Jerusalem was an evil city, filled with sin like a filthy pot encrusted with rust and scum. She had shed innocent blood and hadn't even been decent enough to cover the blood (Gen. 4:10; Lev. 17:13; Deut. 12:16, 24; 15:23). The murderers left the evidence for everyone to see and didn't worry about the consequences! But God would avenge the innocent victims and expose the blood of their murderers for all to see.

—*Be Reverent*, pages 133–34

6. Why were the Jerusalem leaders so confident of deliverance? How did Ezekiel put an end to that delusion? What are examples from our modern church that reflect the same attitude that the Jerusalem leaders had? How can blind arrogance infiltrate a church's leadership? What is the godly way to deal with this kind of leadership?

From the Commentary

It's interesting to study what is said in Scripture about the wives of the prophets. Abraham was a prophet (Gen. 20:7) who twice lied about his wife and got into trouble. Moses was criticized for the wife he chose (Num. 12:1), and Isaiah's wife was a prophetess (Isa. 8:3). She bore him at least two sons whose names were signs to the people of Judah. The prophet Jeremiah wasn't allowed to have a wife (Jer. 16:1–4), and this was a sign to the Jews that judgment was coming and people would wish they had never married and brought children into the world. Hosea's wife became a prostitute and he had to buy her out of the slave market (Hos. 1—3). What a trial that must have been!

But Ezekiel paid a greater price than all these prophets. In order to give his message, Ezekiel had to see his wife die suddenly, *and he was not to show great grief because of it!* God told him that she would suddenly die and that he was not to do what the Jews usually did in times of bereavement. He was allowed to groan quietly, but he was not permitted to weep or make the kind of lamentation that was typical of his people.

He gave his morning message to the elders, at evening his wife suddenly died, and the next morning he buried her.

—*Be Reverent*, page 135

7. Why were the Jews shocked by Ezekiel's response to his wife's sudden death? What explanation did he give them for his unusual actions? How did God use the death of Ezekiel's wife to teach the people a lesson? What does it say about Ezekiel that he was prepared to share that message?

From the Commentary

The destruction of Jerusalem was welcomed by the Gentile nations that were located in the vicinity of the kingdom of Judah. During the great days of their nation, the Jews had been a separated people, and this irritated their neighbors. The Jewish claim that Jehovah was the only true and living God meant that the other nations worshipped only dead idols. Both Saul and David had met many of these nations on the battlefield, and the Gentiles remembered and resented those humiliating defeats. But as the kingdom of Judah drifted from the Lord, the Jewish people adopted the gods and the practices of the Gentiles, and to their neighbors, this looked like pure hypocrisy. After all, if Jehovah is the true and living God, why do the Jews need other gods? And why would the kings of Judah look to human allies for protection if Jehovah is able to care for them? Nothing pleased the Gentiles more than to be able to laugh at the Jews in their day of humiliation and claim that the gods of the Babylonians were stronger than the God the Jews worshipped.

What the nations didn't realize was that the destruction of Jerusalem wasn't just a punishment of the Jews; it was also a warning to the Gentiles. "If the righteous will be recompensed on the earth, how much more the ungodly and the sinner?" (Prov. 11:31 NKJV). For if God displays His wrath against His own people, "What shall the end be of them that obey not the gospel of God?" (1 Peter 4:17). There's a great difference between a loving parent chastening a child and a judge punishing a guilty criminal. Israel knew God's Word and therefore had sinned against a flood of light, but the Gentiles had the clear witness of creation (Rom. 1:18–32; Ps. 19) and conscience (Rom. 2:11–16) and were without excuse. But God was also judging the Gentiles for the way they had treated His people, because this was the covenant promise He had made with Abraham (Gen. 12:1–3).

—*Be Reverent*, pages 139–40

8. Why did God ask Ezekiel to pronounce judgment on the Gentile nations? What does it mean to "set your face against the nations"? (See Ezek. 25:2; 6:2; 13:17; 20:46; 21:2.) What judgments did he declare?

More to Consider: Ezekiel didn't have a message of judgment against the Babylonians. Instead, God used Isaiah (Isa. 13:1—14:23; 21:1–9) and especially Jeremiah (Jer. 50—51) for that job. Why might God have chosen not to let Ezekiel present that particular judgment?

From the Commentary

Having dealt with the sins of the nations related to Israel, Ezekiel then set his face against Philistia (Ezek. 25:15–17) and Phoenicia, especially the Phoenician cities of Tyre (26:1—28:19) and Sidon (vv. 20–24). Once again, the themes of pride, hatred, and revenge come to the fore, sins that can motivate nations even today.

Ezekiel devoted four messages to the sins and the fate of the capital of Phoenicia (Ezek. 26:1–21; 27:1–36; 28:1–10, 11–19). During their reigns, both David and Solomon were friendly with Hiram, king of Tyre (2 Sam. 5:11; 1 Kings 5:1ff.), and King Ahab's wife, Jezebel, was the daughter of Ethbaal, a later king of Tyre (1 Kings 16:31).

—*Be Reverent*, pages 143–44

9. Why did Ezekiel focus on Tyre in his messages? What was prophesied for Tyre? How did Ezekiel describe the city's fate? What was the Jewish nation's response to the fate of Tyre? What spiritual truths did Ezekiel teach to the Jews through this message?

From the Commentary

> One of the major themes of this book is the deliver-
> ance of the Jewish exiles from Babylon and the future
> regathering and reuniting of the nation. After the seventy
> years of exile and the Persian conquest of Babylon, God
> did cause Cyrus to allow the Jewish people to return to
> their land and rebuild the temple (2 Chron. 36:22–23;
> Ezra 1). But the return of about fifty thousand people
> (2:64–65) in 538–537 BC didn't completely fulfill the
> promises in Ezekiel, for they have an application in the
> end times. Certainly the Jewish remnant that returned
> with Zerubbabel didn't "dwell safely" (Ezek. 28:26),
> because they had all kinds of problems with the people
> in the land. Furthermore, Ezekiel mentioned "nations"
> (plural) and not just the one nation of Babylon, where the
> Jews were in exile.
>
> —*Be Reverent*, page 152

10. What was God's promise to the Jews in Ezekiel 28? How would this promise give encouragement to the faithful remnant among the exiles?

Looking Inward

Take a moment to reflect on all that you've explored thus far in this study of Ezekiel 22—28. Review your notes and answers and think about how each of these things matters in your life today.

> *Tips for Small Groups: To get the most out of this section, form pairs or trios and have group members take turns answering these questions. Be honest and as open as you can in this discussion, but most of all, be encouraging and supportive of others. Be sensitive to those who are going through particularly difficult times, and don't press for people to speak if they're uncomfortable doing so.*

11. Have you ever made a list of your past or current sins? Was it easy to review the things you'd done wrong? Why or why not? What did you learn from that experience? If you've never done this, what do you think about the idea of doing it?

12. One of the challenges Ezekiel faced was showing the people why trusting other nations was a mistake—and that they should trust God for help even when it seemed like all hope was lost. Have you ever turned to a source that was not clearly from God for help in solving a problem or

challenge? Why did you make that choice? What fears did you have about God's ability or willingness to help you with the situation? What role did impatience play in your decision to turn away from God for help? What can you learn about your faith from your decision and the results of that choice?

13. God offered the faithful Jews in exile some hope in Ezekiel 28. Think of a time when you were struggling or suffering. How did God show up and offer you hope in the middle of that time? Where do you look for hope when you're going through trying times?

Going Forward

14. Think of one or two things that you have learned that you'd like to work on in the coming week. Remember that this is all about quality, not quantity. It's better to work on one specific area of life and do it well than

to work on many and do poorly (or to be so overwhelmed that you simply don't try).

Do you want to trust God when the odds are stacked against you? Be specific. Go back through Ezekiel 22—28 and put a star next to the phrase or verse that is most encouraging to you. Consider memorizing this verse.

Real-Life Application Ideas: In this chapter, you learned about God's judgment of many nations. Judging is God's business. This week, look for places where you tend to judge others inappropriately. This could be at work, where you judge someone's motives; or at home, where you judge a family member's choices; or even at church. Ask God to reveal those judgmental places in your life and to help you let go of judgment and replace it with love and grace.

Seeking Help

15. Write a prayer below (or simply pray one in silence), inviting God to work on your mind and heart in those areas you've noted in the Going Forward section. Be honest about your desires and fears.

Notes for Small Groups:

- *Look for ways to put into practice the things you wrote in the Going Forward section. Talk with other group members about your ideas and commit to being accountable to one another.*

- *During the coming week, ask the Holy Spirit to continue to reveal truth to you from what you've read and studied.*

- *Before you start the next lesson, read Ezekiel 29—32. For more in-depth lesson preparation, read chapter 9, "Egypt Will Fall!," in* Be Reverent.

Egypt
(EZEKIEL 29—32)

Before you begin ...
- *Pray for the Holy Spirit to reveal truth and wisdom as you go through this lesson.*
- *Read Ezekiel 29—32. This lesson references chapter 9 in* Be Reverent. *It will be helpful for you to have your Bible and a copy of the commentary available as you work through this lesson.*

Getting Started

From the Commentary

Egypt is the seventh nation in Ezekiel's "judgment cycle" and receives more attention than any of the other nations the prophet addressed. Centuries before, Egypt had made the Jewish people suffer greatly as slaves, and even after the division of the Jewish kingdom, the Egyptians were a thorn in the flesh to the Jews and a most undependable ally. But the Jews were like their father Abraham (Gen. 12:10–20) and their ancestors

(Ex. 14:10–12; 16:1–3; Num. 11:4–9, 18; 14:1–5) in that, whenever a crisis loomed, they were prone to look to Egypt for help. The longer the Jews were away from Egypt, the more they idealized their experiences there and forgot about the slavery and the toil. Of course, King Solomon had married an Egyptian princess and did a considerable amount of business with Egypt, but after he died, those bonds began to unravel.

—*Be Reverent*, page 157

1. How was the warning God gave Isaiah in Isaiah 31:1 similar to the message He gave the Jews about Egypt in Ezekiel? Why did the Jews feel compelled to look to Egypt for help? Why was that easier for them to consider than simply trusting God for deliverance?

More to Consider: Ezekiel 29—32 is composed of seven messages (or oracles) that God gave to Ezekiel to deliver to the Egyptians and to the Jewish exiles. Each opens with "the word of the LORD came" or a similar statement. How is it significant that oracles begin with this phrase? How does this phrase validate what's to follow? How would the remnant of faithful Jews respond to that statement? How would the Egyptians?

2. Choose one verse or phrase from Ezekiel 29—32 that stands out to you. This could be something you're intrigued by, something that makes you uncomfortable, something that puzzles you, something that resonates with you, or just something you want to examine further. Write that here.

Going Deeper

From the Commentary

The first message (in Ezekiel 29) was given on January 7, 587 BC, about seven months before Jerusalem was destroyed. The prophet set his face against Pharaoh Hophra, who ruled Egypt from 589 to 570 BC. (See Jer. 44:30.) The picture here is of killing a sea monster.

The Lord compared Hophra to a monster that dwelt in the waters of the river and claimed the river for himself. The Nile River was so essential to the life of Egypt that it was treated like a god, but Hophra claimed that he was the one who made the river and that it belonged to him. In this oracle, Pharaoh was compared to a ferocious crocodile, guarding the waters of the land—the Nile and all the canals—and attacking anybody who dared to challenge his claims. His major sin was pride (Ezek. 29:1–5), taking credit for what the Lord God had done. Whatever greatness belonged to Egypt, it was because of the gracious gifts of God and not because of what Pharaoh and his people had accomplished.

But the Lord wasn't impressed by the crocodile or afraid of him! He promised to catch him, put hooks in his mouth, and drag him and the fish clinging to him (the people of Egypt) out to the fields where they would be exposed to the sun and die. They would become food for the beasts of the field and the carrion-eating birds.

—*Be Reverent*, page 158

3. Why did God choose a crocodile as the image to use for Pharaoh Hophra? What was the purpose of such a vivid and brutal description of the crocodile's defeat? How would the exiles have received this part of the prophecy? Why would the kind of death predicted in this prophecy have been an affront to the pharaoh?

From the Commentary

Ezekiel 29:8–12 includes the prophecy of the coming of the Babylonian army to Egypt, where they would fulfill God's word and destroy man and beast as well as ravage the land (Jer. 43:8–13; 46). The people would either be slain or scattered, and the land would be left "utterly waste and desolate" (Ezek. 29:10). The phrase in verse 10, "From the tower of Syene even unto the border of Ethiopia" is the Egyptian equivalent of Israel's "from Dan to Beersheba" and signifies the whole land, from top to bottom. The NIV translates it "from Migdol [in the north] to Aswan [in the south]." Nebuchadnezzar would make a clean sweep of the land, and the desolation would last forty years (vv. 11–13). Nebuchadnezzar attacked Egypt in 568–567 BC and fulfilled that prophecy.

After forty years, the Lord would (1) regather the scattered Egyptians to their land and permit them to establish their kingdom, but (2) their kingdom would not regain its former power and glory. It would become a "base kingdom." The Jews would learn that Egypt couldn't be trusted and would not put their confidence in Egypt.

—*Be Reverent*, page 159

4. What does the way God took care of the Egyptians reveal about how He orders the world to effect His purposes and plan? What lessons did God teach the Egyptians? What message did He give His people by the way He changed the Egyptians' story?

From Today's World

When Christianity becomes profitable, big secular companies take notice. This is the trend in such industries as book publishing and music production, but it's not limited to those industries. There's a hunger in our world for resources that preach a message of hope, and for better or worse, that hunger means there's also a market for products serving the need. Seeing the potential for profit, large secular companies aren't shy to step in and offer their vast resources in exchange for purchasing a stake in a Christian company (or buying it outright). This isn't a new trend, but the more people show interest in spending money on Christian media, the more secular companies will see that as an opportunity.

5. How is the relationship between Christian companies and secular companies today similar to that of the Jews and their affection for countries like Egypt in Ezekiel's day? What are the advantages of allying with a larger company, whether or not that company espouses the same values? What are the challenges? What are some parallels to this kind of relationship on a smaller, more personal scale? What's most important to keep in mind when you're considering allying yourself with someone who may not share the same beliefs?

From the Commentary

The second oracle (Ezek. 29:17–21) was given April 26, 571 BC, which is the latest date mentioned in the book of Ezekiel. However, the prophet included it here because it related to Egypt. Since Nebuchadnezzar was a servant of the Lord (Jer. 25:9; 27:6; 43:10), he deserved his pay, but the spoils of war from the conquest of Tyre couldn't begin to compensate him for the time and work his army put into the siege. ("Great service" in Ezek. 29:18 NIV is "hard campaign.") They spent fifteen years building ramparts and attacking Tyre, but they couldn't prevent the city from using their large navy to transport their treasures elsewhere. Egypt had even assisted the people of Tyre in resisting the attack and relocating their wealth.

God determined that Egypt should provide the wages for the Babylonian army that had grown bald and bruised during the siege. God is sovereign over the nations and can accomplish His will without destroying either their freedom or their accountability to Him. In 568 BC, Nebuchadnezzar did invade Egypt, sweeping through the country and leaving it desolate (see vv. 8–12). Thus God punished both Tyre and Egypt and rewarded Babylon.

—*Be Reverent*, page 160

6. What does all this have to do with God's people, Israel? What message did God's decision about repayment by Egypt send to the Jews? What is the word of promise Ezekiel added for the Jews? (See Ezek. 29:21.) Why

was the theme of restoration so valuable to the Jews at this time? Why is it so important for us even today?

From the Commentary

The third oracle (Ezek. 30:1–19) isn't dated but was probably delivered about the same time as the previous one. It pictures the judgment of Egypt in terms of a great storm that shakes the very foundations of the land.

"The day of the LORD" (v. 3) is a biblical phrase that describes any period of divine judgment, such as the judgment of Egypt. It particularly refers to the time of tribulation in the last days when the Lord will punish the nations (Isa. 65:17–19; Joel 1—3; Zeph. 1—2; Rev. 6—19) before He returns to earth to establish His kingdom. Whether this judgment is local, as with Egypt, or global, as in the last days, it is the Lord's work, and nobody can stop it or control it. It is "a day of clouds, a time of doom for the nations" (Ezek. 30:3 NIV). In the end times, all the nations will experience this time of wrath, but in Ezekiel's time, judgment would fall on Egypt and her neighboring allies. This would include Ethiopia (Cush, the upper Nile region; see vv. 5, 9), Put (an African nation), Lud (Lydia), the Arabian nations, Cub (Libya), and "the people of the covenant" (v. 5 NIV), who are probably Jews serving as mercenaries in the Egyptian army (see 27:10).

When the Babylon sword invades the land, not only will Egypt fall, but so will their allies. Those areas were desolate enough before, but now they would be even worse as the land is devastated. God will crush Egypt's allies and light a fire that will destroy the land. The people of Cush will think they are secure, so the Lord will send them messengers to wake them up, but it will be too late.

When the Lord punished Egypt during the time of Israel's slavery, He did the work Himself; but now He would use Nebuchadnezzar as His appointed servant to punish the proud Egyptians. His army would be ruthless (28:7, "terrible" KJV; see 31:12; 32:12) and fill the land with corpses. But His judgments would also affect the rivers and make them dry, a great catastrophe for such an arid land.

Ezekiel has told us what would happen and how it would happen, and now he reveals the vast scope of God's wrath. Note the repetition of the phrase "I will" as the Lord describes His work of judgment in both Lower Egypt ("Noph" = "Memphis," Ezek. 30:13) and Upper Egypt (Pathros). Instead of a land of pride, Egypt will be a land filled with fear. "Zoan" is "Rameses," "No" is "Thebes," and "Sin" is "Pelusium." The verbs used make it clear that the Lord will permit total devastation: destroy, make desolate, set fire, pour fury, cut off, the day darkened.

The Jews were led out of Egypt by a bright cloud (Ex. 13:21), but the Egyptians who once enslaved them will be under a dark cloud. As a result of God's judgment, the power and pride of Egypt will be destroyed, and the nation would never rise to its former heights again. The young men would be slain and the young women taken into slavery, so the future generation would be given into the hands of the enemy.

—*Be Reverent*, pages 161–62

7. Why is pride such a dangerous sin? Why did God use Nebuchadnezzar to punish the Egyptians for their pride? What does this reveal about God's character? What unexpected means does God use to accomplish His goals today? Why do the nations never seem to learn that God will always get His way? What does this say about humankind?

From the Commentary

The oracle in Ezekiel 30:20–26 was delivered on April 29, 587 BC, and refers to God's crushing the Egyptian military power. The arm is a symbol of power, but God would break both of Pharaoh's arms and leave Egypt helpless. Nobody would apply splints or even bandage up the wounds to promote healing.

The first "breaking" took place at Carchemish in 605 BC, when Nebuchadnezzar defeated Pharaoh Necho (2 Kings 24:7; Jer. 46:2). It was also at Carchemish that godly King Josiah was slain. The second "breaking" occurred when Pharaoh Hophra tried to help Judah when Nebuchadnezzar attacked Jerusalem (37:5ff.). With both arms "broken," Egypt would not be able to wield a sword, and that would put an end to the battle. Pharaoh Hophra had a second title, "The Strong-Armed," but that title would not apply anymore.

While the Lord was permitting the Babylonians to break the arms of Egypt, He was also strengthening the arms of the Babylonians! He even put His own sword into the hand of Nebuchadnezzar! The Egyptians would be either slain or scattered and their land would be left desolate. "They shall know that I am the LORD" is repeated twice (Ezek. 30:25–26).

—*Be Reverent*, page 163

8. Why was it so important that the Egyptians know the true God if the pharaoh wasn't about to change his beliefs? What would the Egyptians learn through this defeat, especially considering that God used the Babylonians—the people who were holding His people in exile—to make it happen? Do we see examples of this kind of show of God's power in today's world? Why or why not?

More to Consider: The cedars in Lebanon were widely known for their quality and their height. Assyria was like one of those cedars, impressive in height and expansive in growth. It was nurtured by many waters, which symbolize the nations under Assyria's control that contributed to her wealth. (These nations are also symbolized by the fowl and the beasts that had security because of the tree.) Why did the Lord allow Assyria to achieve greatness? Why did He use their power in response to the northern kingdom's rebellion (while protecting Jerusalem from them at the same time)? (See Isa. 37; 2 Kings 19; 2 Chron. 32.) How did this once again reveal God's sovereign power?

From the Commentary

The date of the oracle in Ezekiel 32:1–16 is March 5, 585 BC, two months after the exiles in Babylon received the news that Jerusalem had fallen (33:21–22). The "monster" theme was used in 29:1–16, but Ezekiel uses it again to bring out some additional spiritual truths.

Ezekiel 32:1–10 is an "official lamentation" for the king of Egypt who thought he was a great lion but in God's sight was only a crocodile. Pharaoh thrashed about in the water and made a big scene, but all he did was muddy the waters and create problems by disobeying the Lord.

In chapter 29, God caught the Egyptian crocodile with a hook, but now Egypt is so weak, it can be easily caught with a net. (See 12:13; 17:20; 19:8.) God would take the crocodile to the land and leave him there to die, and the vultures would devour the carcass, reminding us of

29:3–5. But he adds two more images: the land drenched in blood and the heavens shrouded in darkness (32:6–8). These are reminders of the first and ninth plagues before Israel's exodus from Egypt: the turning of the water into blood and the darkness for three days (Ex. 7:20–24; 10:21–29). According to Revelation 8:8–9, a similar judgment will fall during the great tribulation.

—*Be Reverent*, page 166

9. Read Joel 3; Amos 5:18–20; and Matthew 24. How are the images in these passages similar to the images described in Ezekiel 32:1–16? In what ways were the events in Egypt a dress rehearsal for the judgments of the last days?

From the Commentary

The seventh oracle is found in Ezekiel 32:17–32, and since no other date is recorded, we assume it was given two weeks after the previous message—March 17, 585 BC. It follows the style of 31:15–18 and describes the people of Egypt descending into sheol, the world of the dead.

Ezekiel was instructed to wail because of the multitudes of people who would be slain by the swords of the Babylonians.

The picture is grim and almost macabre as the other nations welcome Pharaoh and his hosts and taunt them as they arrive in the underworld. We might paraphrase their words, "So you thought you were so beautiful and strong? Look at you now! You prided yourselves in being a circumcised people, but now you are lying down in death with the uncircumcised. Like us, you thought you were invincible, but now you have joined us in death and decay. You are no longer on a throne—you are in a grave! Your bed is a sepulchre."

Like the king of Assyria before him (31:16), Pharaoh would see all these princes and common people and be comforted that he wasn't the only one defeated and slain.

—*Be Reverent*, pages 167–68

10. Why did God deliver such a grim and macabre picture in this message to Egypt? Why would the pharaoh have received "comfort" that he wasn't the only one in sheol who had been defeated? How does the phrase "death is the great leveler" apply to the theme of this oracle? Read 1 Corinthians 15:55–57. How does this passage give believers hope over death?

Looking Inward

Take a moment to reflect on all that you've explored thus far in this study of Ezekiel 29—32. Review your notes and answers and think about how each of these things matters in your life today.

> *Tips for Small Groups: To get the most out of this section, form pairs or trios and have group members take turns answering these questions. Be honest and as open as you can in this discussion, but most of all, be encouraging and supportive of others. Be sensitive to those who are going through particularly difficult times, and don't press for people to speak if they're uncomfortable doing so.*

11. One of God's messages to His people was about restoration. What does restoration mean to you? Have you experienced it? Describe what that was like. What are some areas of your life where you are still hoping, praying for restoration?

12. Pride is a common theme in biblical history. It always seems to be at the core of a nation's failures. How have you struggled with pride? Why is it so difficult to let go of pride? How is humility a form of strength rather

than weakness? Describe a time when you were able to let go of pride and trust God's way, even though it may have seemed difficult.

13. Many of the images in Ezekiel's prophecies are brutally vivid. What is your reaction to these parts of Scripture? What purpose do these descriptions serve to the church in general? How do they affect the way you view God? How do they affect the way you relate to the world?

Going Forward

14. Think of one or two things that you have learned that you'd like to work on in the coming week. Remember that this is all about quality, not quantity. It's better to work on one specific area of life and do it well than to work on many and do poorly (or to be so overwhelmed that you simply don't try).

Do you want to pray for restoration? Be specific. Go back through Ezekiel 29—32 and put a star next to the phrase or verse that is most encouraging to you. Consider memorizing this verse.

Real-Life Application Ideas: This week, focus on practical acts of restoration. This can include actual, physical restoration (such as refinishing that deck you've been meaning to get to for years) and social or emotional restoration (healing a broken relationship, for example). Focus on making things right or making things better. In all of these things, seek God's heart before you begin; then thank Him for modeling the very idea of restoration in history and, most notably, the sacrifice of His Son on the cross.

Seeking Help

15. Write a prayer below (or simply pray one in silence), inviting God to work on your mind and heart in those areas you've noted in the Going Forward section. Be honest about your desires and fears.

Notes for Small Groups:

- *Look for ways to put into practice the things you wrote in the Going Forward section. Talk with other group members about your ideas and commit to being accountable to one another.*

- *During the coming week, ask the Holy Spirit to continue to reveal truth to you from what you've read and studied.*

- *Before you start the next lesson, read Ezekiel 33—37. For more in-depth lesson preparation, read chapters 10 and 11, "Warnings and Promises from the Watchman" and "From Restoration to Reunion," in* Be Reverent.

Warnings and Promises
(EZEKIEL 33—37)

Before you begin …
- *Pray for the Holy Spirit to reveal truth and wisdom as you go through this lesson.*
- *Read Ezekiel 33—37. This lesson references chapters 10 and 11 in* Be Reverent. *It will be helpful for you to have your Bible and a copy of the commentary available as you work through this lesson.*

Getting Started

From the Commentary

Ezekiel 33 reaches back into some of Ezekiel's previous messages and brings together truths that were important to Israel's understanding of God, their situation, and what God wanted them to do. You will find here references to 3:15–27; chapters 5 and 6; 11:14–21; 18:1–32; 20:1–8; and 24:25–27. It's as though the Lord led His servant to combine these basic spiritual truths in one message so that nobody could say, "I didn't hear what the Lord said to us!" Ezekiel turned the light of God's Word on the nation as a whole (33:1–20), the people left in Judah and Jerusalem (vv. 23–29), and the exiles in Babylon (vv. 21–22, 30–33).

—*Be Reverent*, pages 173–74

1. In chapter 33, what did Ezekiel reveal about what was in the people's hearts? What did he say about human responsibility before God? In what ways did he speak to anguish, regret, remorse, and repentance?

More to Consider: When Peter remembered his sin of denying Christ, he repented and sought pardon; when Judas remembered his sin of betraying Christ, he experienced only remorse, and he went out and hanged himself. "Godly sorrow brings repentance that leads to salvation and leaves no regret, but worldly sorrow brings death" (2 Cor. 7:10). If the sinner turns from his sins and turns to the Lord in faith, he will be forgiven. Paul's message was, "Turn to God in repentance and have faith in our Lord Jesus" (Acts 20:21), and that message is still valid today.

2. Choose one verse or phrase from Ezekiel 33—37 that stands out to you. This could be something you're intrigued by, something that makes you uncomfortable, something that puzzles you, something that resonates with you, or just something you want to examine further. Write that here.

Going Deeper

From the Commentary

> Ezekiel had already exposed the sins of the nation's leaders (chap. 22), but he returned to this theme in chapter 34 because it had a bearing on Israel's future. While this message applied to Israel's current situation in Ezekiel's day, it also has application in that future day when the Lord gathers His scattered people back to their land. This message certainly must have brought hope to the exiles as they realized the Lord had not forsaken them but would care for them as a shepherd for his sheep.

> When the Lord spoke about "the flock," He was referring to the nation of Israel (34:31). "We are his people, and the sheep of his pasture" (Ps. 100:3; see 77:20; 78:52; 80:1). Moses saw Israel as a flock (Num. 27:17; see 1 Kings 22:17) and so did Jeremiah (Jer. 13:17) and Zechariah

(Zech. 10:3). Jesus spoke of "the lost sheep of the house of Israel" (Matt. 10:6; 15:24). Because Jesus called Himself "the Good Shepherd" and "the door of the sheep" (John 10:7, 11), the image of the flock carried over into the church (Acts 20:28–29; 1 Peter 5:2–3). Our English word *pastor* comes from the Latin and means "shepherd."

—*Be Reverent*, pages 178–79

3. What was the "flock" the Lord spoke about in Ezekiel 34? (See also Ps. 77:20; 78:52; 80:1; 100:3.) What are the connotations of the word *flock*? How did God use this description again in the New Testament? (See John 10:7, 11; Acts 20:28–29; 1 Peter 5:2–3.)

From the Commentary

Was there any hope for God's scattered people? Yes, because the Lord would come to deliver His flock from their oppressors and gather them to Himself. In Ezekiel's time, the Lord brought His people back from Babylon, but the picture here is certainly much broader than that, for the Lord spoke about "countries" (Ezek. 34:13). Ezekiel promises that in the end times, the Lord will gather His flock "from all places where they have been scattered" (v. 12) and bring them back to their own land where He will be their shepherd (Matt. 24:31).

—*Be Reverent*, pages 179–80

4. Why might people apply this prophecy to the return of the remnant after their exile in Babylon? What is behind the temptation to spiritualize it and apply it to the church today? If the prophet was speaking about a literal future regathering of Israel (see Ezek. 11:17; 20:34, 41–42; 28:25; 36:24; 37:21–25; 38:8), what does that teach us about God's covenant and about God's character? (See Deut. 30:1–10; Isa. 11:11–12; Jer. 23:3–8; Mic. 2:12; 4:6–8.)

From the Commentary

The Lord promised that the people would be safe in the land and not be oppressed by the peoples around them. Except during the reigns of David and Solomon, the nation of Israel has been attacked, conquered, and ravaged by one nation after another, but this will cease when

Messiah is on the throne. A "covenant of peace" would govern the land (Ezek. 34:25; see 37:26), which probably refers to the new covenant that Jeremiah promised in Jeremiah 31:31–34. The law of God would be written on the hearts of the people and they all would know the Lord and obey His will.

—*Be Reverent*, page 181

5. In what ways had Ezekiel watched the glory of God leave the temple? (See Ezek. 11:22–23.) How would he also see God's glory return? (See 43:1–5.) What does this chapter in the history of God's people teach us about God's patience? God's insistence on obedience? God's love?

From the Commentary

The Lord had already pronounced judgment on Edom through Isaiah (Isa. 34; 63:1–6), Jeremiah (Jer. 49:7–22), and Ezekiel (Ezek. 25:12–14), but now He did it again and added some details (see Ezek. 35:1–15). Mount Seir is another name for Edom, the nation founded by Esau, Jacob's twin brother. "Edom" means "red" and was a nickname given to Esau (Gen. 25:30). Esau was a man of the world who had no spiritual desires and willingly sold his birthright to his brother Jacob. Esau fought with his brother even in their mother's womb (vv. 21–26) and hated his brother because the Lord had chosen Jacob to receive the blessings of the covenant. This hatred was passed on from generation to generation and the Edomites maintained what God called "a perpetual hatred" (Ezek. 35:5; 25:15; Amos 1:11–12; Obad.). This hatred was no doubt like some of the "ethnic wars" that the world has seen today.

—*Be Reverent*, pages 181–82

6. What was the Edomites' great sin? How was their role in assisting Babylon's attack of the Jews a mirror of their founder's (Esau's) actions? Why did the Edomites hate Israel? What was God's judgment against Edom? Was this a just judgment? Explain.

From the Commentary

"Our hope is lost!" That's what the Jewish exiles were saying to one another as they "pined away" in Babylon (Ezek. 37:11; 33:10), and from the human point of view, the statement was true. But if they had listened to their prophets, they would have had hope in the Lord and looked forward with anticipation. Jeremiah had written to them that they would be in Babylon for seventy years, and that God's thoughts toward them were of peace and not of evil (Jer. 29:10). Ezekiel had given them God's promise that He would gather His people and take them back to their land (Ezek. 11:17; 20:34, 41–42; 28:25). A Latin proverb says, "Where there is life, there is hope," but the reverse is also true: Where there is hope, we find reason to live. Swiss theologian Emil Brunner wrote, "What oxygen is to the lungs, such is hope for the meaning of life."

In his previous messages, Ezekiel looked back and reproved the people because of their sins. Now he looks ahead and encourages the people.

—*Be Reverent*, page 187

7. How did Ezekiel encourage the people about their future? What promises did he offer them? How does each of the following words apply to the future of Israel as presented by Ezekiel: *restoration, regeneration, resurrection, reunion*?

From the Commentary

God gave the land of Israel to the Jews as a part of the Abrahamic covenant (Gen. 12:1–3; 13:14–18; 15:7–21). That settled their *ownership* of the land, but their *possession* and *enjoyment* of the land depended on their faith and obedience (Lev. 26). The Christian life is similar. We *enter* God's family by trusting Jesus Christ (John 3:16; Eph. 2:8–9), but we *enjoy* God's family by believing His promises and obeying His will (2 Cor. 6:18—7:1). Disobedient children have to be chastened (Heb. 12), and God often had to chasten the people of Israel because of their rebellion and disobedience.

Ezekiel had set his face against Mount Seir, which represented the land of Edom (Ezek. 35), but now he addressed "the mountains of Israel" as representative of the land of Israel. The Babylonians had ravaged and plundered the Promised Land, and the neighboring nations (especially Edom) had tried to possess the land (35:10). Instead of assisting the Jews, the neighbors had ridiculed them and even helped the Babylonians loot the city of Jerusalem. Why? Because of their long-standing hatred of the Jews and a desire to possess the land of Israel. "Aha, even the ancient high places are ours in possession" (36:2).

—Be Reverent, page 188

8. Review Ezekiel 36:1–15. What is the purpose of the word "therefore" in this section? Why is it used so often? What were the promised consequences for the enemies of God's people?

More to Consider: The Jews were separated from their temple, now destroyed, and from the things necessary for Jewish worship, but the Lord was still with them and could see their hearts. The Jews had profaned God's name by defiling the sanctuary (Ezek. 5:11; 22:26), but He had promised to be a sanctuary for them in Babylon (11:16). They had profaned the Sabbaths (22:8; 23:38), but they knew what day it was in Babylon and could still seek to obey God. How is the church today similar to the exiled Jews? In what ways are we "in exile" in our own land? How can we still count on God no matter what the world around us says or asks of us?

From the Commentary

Ezekiel has told the people the Lord's promise to restore the land and regenerate His people. But what about the nation itself, a nation divided (Israel and Judah) and without a king or a temple? The remnant would return to the ravaged land and rebuild the temple and the city, but none of the blessings Ezekiel promised would come to them at that time. No, the prophet Ezekiel was looking far down the corridor of time to the end of the age when Jesus the Messiah would return and claim His people. Ezekiel told the people that the dead nation would one day be raised to life, and the divided nation would be united!

At the beginning of Ezekiel's ministry, the Spirit transported him to sit among the discouraged exiles by the canal (Ezek. 3:14ff.). Later, the Spirit took him in visions to Jerusalem (8:3ff.), to the temple gate, and then back to Babylon (11:1, 24). Now the Spirit brought him in a vision to a valley filled with many bleached bones scattered on the ground, the skeletons of corpses long ago decomposed and devoured by carrion-eating birds and animals. These people were slain (37:9), and they may have been soldiers in the Jewish army (v. 10).

It was a humiliating thing for the body of a dead Jew not to be washed, wrapped, and buried with dignity in a grave or a tomb. These bodies were left on the battlefield to become food for the vultures to eat and objects for the sun to bleach. But the Lord had warned Israel in the covenant He made with them that their sins would lead to just that kind of shameful experience. "The LORD will cause you to be defeated before your enemies.... Your carcasses shall be food for all the birds of the air and the beasts of the earth, and no one shall frighten them away"

(Deut. 28:25–26 NKJV). Jeremiah was preaching this same message in Jerusalem: "I [the Lord] will give them into the hand of their enemies and into the hand of those who seek their life. Their dead bodies shall be for meat for the birds of the heaven and the beasts of the earth" (Jer. 34:20 NKJV).

—*Be Reverent*, page 195

9. Review Ezekiel 37:1–14. What was the purpose of this vision of dry bones? What was Ezekiel's reply to God's question about the bones? What was the promise God had hidden in the answer? (See also Rom. 4:17.)

From the Commentary

The nation of Israel was a united people until after the death of Solomon. His son's unwise and arrogant policies divided the kingdom in 931 BC, with ten tribes forming the northern kingdom of Israel (also called Ephraim or Samaria) and the tribes of Judah and Benjamin forming the southern kingdom of Judah. The northern kingdom soon went into idolatry and apostasy and in 722 BC was taken by Assyria, but Judah had some good kings and maintained the Davidic line and the ministry at the temple. However, toward the end of Israel's political history, some very weak kings reigned, and the nation drifted into idolatry and unbelief. The Lord finally brought the Babylonians to chasten His people. There is a political Israel today, but the majority of the Jewish people are scattered around the world.

—*Be Reverent*, pages 197–98

10. Review Ezekiel 37:15–28. What is the theme of this action sermon? How was the people's response similar to the way Jesus' disciples often responded to His parables? Why was the message of unity so important to the people? What would maintain that unity?

Looking Inward

Take a moment to reflect on all that you've explored thus far in this study of Ezekiel 33—37. Review your notes and answers and think about how each of these things matters in your life today.

Tips for Small Groups: To get the most out of this section, form pairs or trios and have group members take turns answering these questions. Be honest and as open as you can in this discussion, but most of all, be encouraging and supportive of others. Be sensitive to those who are going through particularly difficult times, and don't press for people to speak if they're uncomfortable doing so.

11. Have you ever tried to claim the "But I didn't know that!" defense when confronted with a sin you'd committed? Why was it so difficult to accept responsibility for your actions? What was the road you took back to humility and acceptance of your actions? What can you do in the future to avoid letting pride or embarrassment get in the way of acknowledging the truth, no matter how ugly that truth might be?

12. When have you pined away with the lament "hope is lost"? What prompted that season of hopelessness? What was God's ultimate answer to your feeling? What did you discover about yourself through that experience? About God?

13. God's promises were often for events long down the road of history. The people who heard the promises wouldn't live to see them fulfilled. What are some of God's promises that you hope to see fulfilled in your lifetime? What are some you expect you may not see? Does it matter to you if you live to see all those promises fulfilled? Why or why not?

Going Forward

14. Think of one or two things that you have learned that you'd like to work on in the coming week. Remember that this is all about quality, not quantity. It's better to work on one specific area of life and do it well than to work on many and do poorly (or to be so overwhelmed that you simply don't try).

Do you want to lament in a godly way? Be specific. Go back through

Ezekiel 33—37 and put a star next to the phrase or verse that is most encouraging to you. Consider memorizing this verse.

Real-Life Application Ideas: This week, take some time to focus on the future promises of God. Consider all the things that He will make right in the fulfillment of His plan—no more hunger, no more death, etc. Thank God for these promises; then ask Him how you can act in the now to bring some of those kingdom promises into people's lives today. Maybe that's simply a matter of sharing with others the hope of tomorrow, or perhaps you can take some practical actions to show one of God's promises to another person today. Certainly there are hungry people in your community—can you help to feed them? Bring the kingdom truths to life today while enjoying the promise of even greater truths for tomorrow.

Seeking Help

15. Write a prayer below (or simply pray one in silence), inviting God to work on your mind and heart in those areas you've noted in the Going Forward section. Be honest about your desires and fears.

Notes for Small Groups:

- *Look for ways to put into practice the things you wrote in the Going Forward section. Talk with other group members about your ideas and commit to being accountable to one another.*

- *During the coming week, ask the Holy Spirit to continue to reveal truth to you from what you've read and studied.*

- *Before you start the next lesson, read Ezekiel 38—48. For more in-depth lesson preparation, read chapters 12 and 13, "God Protects the Nation" and "Glory in the Temple," in* Be Reverent.

Protection and Glory

(Ezekiel 38—48)

Before you begin …
- *Pray for the Holy Spirit to reveal truth and wisdom as you go through this lesson.*
- *Read Ezekiel 38—48. This lesson references chapters 12 and 13 in* Be Reverent. *It will be helpful for you to have your Bible and a copy of the commentary available as you work through this lesson.*

Getting Started

From the Commentary

Before we examine Ezekiel 38—39, we should consider the book of Revelation and review the prophetic situation prior to this invasion of the Holy Land. The next crisis event on God's prophetic calendar is the rapture of the church, an event that can occur at any time (1 Thess. 4:13–18). Jesus Christ will come in the air and call His people to be with Him in heaven. According to Daniel 9:24–27, the nation of Israel will make an agreement with the head of a ten-nation European coalition to protect them for seven years so they can rebuild their temple in Jerusalem. *We don't know how much time elapses between the rapture of the church and the signing of this covenant.* It's the signing of the covenant that triggers the start of the seven-year tribulation period described in Matthew 24:1–28 and Revelation 6—19.

After three and one-half years, this European leader will emerge as the Antichrist (the Beast). He will break the covenant with Israel, set up his own image in the Jewish temple, and try to force the world to worship and obey him (Dan. 9:27; 2 Thess. 2:1–12; Matt. 24:15; Rev. 13). During the last three and one-half years of the tribulation period, the world will experience "the wrath of God," and the period will climax with the return of Christ to the earth to defeat Satan and the Beast and establish His kingdom. That's when the battle of Armageddon will be fought.

If this is the correct sequence of prophetic events, then during the first half of the tribulation period, Israel will be in her land, protected by the strongest political leader in the world. It will be a time of peace and safety when the other nations won't threaten them (Ezek. 38:8, 11, 14). Since we don't know how much time will elapse between the rapture of the church and the signing of the covenant, it's possible that the Jews and this powerful European leader will complete their negotiations very soon after the saints have been taken out. We don't know how long it will take for Israel to rebuild the temple, but it will be complete by the middle of this seven-year period. That's when this powerful European leader will break the covenant, reveal himself as the man of sin, and set up his own image in the temple.

—*Be Reverent*, pages 204–5

1. Why is the discussion of the end times still such a contentious subject among Christians? How does analyzing the words in books like Ezekiel and Revelation help us prepare for an uncertain future? How do sometimes-cryptic messages and images help us today?

More to Consider: The leader of the army in Ezekiel 38 is named Gog, ruler of Magog, which means "the land of Gog." It was located between the Black Sea and the Caspian Sea. The title "chief prince" can be translated "prince of Rosh," a place that hasn't been determined yet. But if "prince of Rosh" is the correct translation, then this man will rule over Rosh, Meshech, and Tubal. The latter two places are located in eastern Asia Minor along with Gomer and Beth Togarmah. Prince Gog's allies will be Persia (Iran), Cush (ancient Ethiopia), Put (Libya), Gomer, and Beth Togarmah, located near the Black Sea. Since all these nations except Put, Cush, and Persia are located north of Israel, it's tempting to identify Rosh with Russia and therefore Meshech with Moscow and Tubal with Tobolsk, both cities in Russia. Why is it risky to make such a leap of logic? What can be gained through this sort of interpretation? What are the risks? What does this sort of detail in Scripture teach us about the challenges of interpretation, particularly when it comes to future events? What is God's ultimate role in the events described in Ezekiel 38—39? What general truth can we take away from this, rather than trying to match the places in Scripture with modern geography?

2. Choose one verse or phrase from Ezekiel 38—48 that stands out to you. This could be something you're intrigued by, something that makes you uncomfortable, something that puzzles you, something that resonates with you, or just something you want to examine further. Write that here.

Going Deeper

From the Commentary

The description of the defeat in Ezekiel 38 focuses on the army, but in 39:1–8, the focus is on the leader of the army, Prince Gog of Magog. In the KJV, verse 2 gives the impression that one sixth of the invading army will be spared and sent home humiliated. However, the verse is stating that it is God who brings Prince Gog into the land and allows him to try to attack the people of Israel.

God not only leads the prince, but He also disarms him so that he is helpless before his enemy (v. 3). Instead of slaughtering the Jews, his soldiers will themselves be slaughtered and become food for the vultures and the beasts of the field. But the Lord won't stop with His judgment of the armies that invade Israel; He will also send a fiery judgment on the land of Magog (v. 6)!

—*Be Reverent*, pages 207–8

3. What reasons for bringing Gog and his armies to Israel (and then defeating them) did the Lord give in Ezekiel 39:23? How did God repeatedly reveal His greatness to the nations? His holiness? What did He ask of the people when He revealed Himself in these ways? How is this true even today?

From the Commentary

The sudden destruction of a great army will leave behind a multitude of corpses as well as a huge amount of military material. We aren't told how much other damage was done by the storm God sent, but it's clear that the land needed cleaning up.

People from the cities of Israel will go out and gather and burn the weapons and supplies left by Gog's defeated army. The ancient military equipment listed here includes hand shields and body shields (bucklers), bows and arrows, and clubs and spears. These are not the weapons of a modern army, but Ezekiel used language the people could understand. If he had written about jet planes and rockets, he would have been a poor communicator. So large will be the collection of unused equipment that the people will use it for fuel for seven years.

But supposing these were actually wooden weapons, would they last that long? Could that many people heat their homes, factories, and businesses for seven years by burning bows and arrows, clubs and spears and shields? And will the people in Israel at that future time be heating the buildings with fireplaces and wood-burning stoves? Wouldn't the dead soldiers ceremonially defile most of this equipment? The burning of the equipment simply says that the Jews didn't keep it to use themselves and they destroyed it so nobody else could use it. Gog and his army came to spoil Israel, but Israel spoiled them!

—*Be Reverent*, page 209

4. Why did the land have to be cleansed? What were the practical reasons for this? The spiritual reasons? What lessons can we learn today from the importance given to cleansing in the time of Ezekiel?

From Today's World

The people in Ezekiel's time were both disappointed by their circumstances and hopeful for a better future. They would have heard God's message both as an immediate answer to their circumstance and perhaps also as a promise of something much further down the road. Today's church is not so different from God's people during this time in history. We are often searching for God's intervention in the now—for answers to cultural and political and social problems facing God's people, and the world at large, while also hanging on to the promises of a "new earth" after Jesus returns. There is a tension between holding on to the hope of God's action in the now and the promise of it in the future. And this is often the point where churches, and their members, struggle most. Just as God's people in history did.

5. Why is it important to hold on to the promise of God's intervention in the future? How can Christians today keep that future hope in balance with living in the now? What does this tension between the now and the

not yet reveal about God's character? About our own? How are we like and unlike the Jews during their time of exile?

From the Commentary

> Ezekiel has described the return of the Jewish people to their land, the cleansing of the nation, and the restoring of the land to productivity and security. But for the picture to be complete, he must give them assurance that their beloved temple and its ministries will be restored, for the presence of God's glory in the temple was what set Israel apart from all the nations (Rom. 9:4).
>
> —*Be Reverent*, page 215

6. Why was the temple so important to the Jewish people as they considered their eventual return to their Promised Land? Why did Ezekiel spend so much effort (nine chapters) describing the new temple and its new ministries? How would this detail have provided hope to the people?

From the Commentary

There are two temples in Israel's future: the tribulation temple, which will be taken over by the Antichrist (Dan. 9:24, 26–27; Matt. 24:15; 2 Thess. 2:1–4), and the millennial temple described in Ezekiel 40—48 (Rev. 11:1; 15:5). But Ezekiel isn't the only prophet who said there would be a holy temple during the kingdom age. You find a kingdom temple and kingdom worship mentioned in Isaiah 2:1–5; 60:7, 13; Jeremiah 33:18; Joel 3:18; Micah 4:2; Haggai 2:7–9; and Zechariah 6:12–15; 14:16, 20–21. Ezekiel 37:24–28 records God's promise to His people that He would put His sanctuary among them. "My tabernacle also shall be with them; indeed, I will be their God, and they shall be My people" (v. 27 NKJV).

God gave the plans for the tabernacle to Moses, a prophet (Ex. 25:8–9, 40), and the plans for Solomon's temple to David, a king (1 Chron. 28:11–19). Now He reveals the plans for the glorious millennial temple to Ezekiel, who was a priest as well as a prophet. These plans had a direct bearing on the people to whom Ezekiel was ministering, discouraged Jews who in the Babylonian siege had lost their land, their Holy City, their temple, and many of their loved ones. In these closing chapters of his prophecy, Ezekiel assured them that God would keep His covenant promises and one day dwell again with His chosen people.

—*Be Reverent*, page 219

7. How does a literal interpretation of these visions help our understanding of the word God gave Ezekiel? Why is a figurative interpretation more complicated to understand? Is it necessary to know the figurative implications of a vision in order to get the main message? Explain.

From the Commentary

It was on April 28, 573 BC—the first day of Passover—that God gave Ezekiel the vision recorded in chapters 40—48. The Jews had been captives in Babylon for twenty-five years, and Passover would only remind them of their deliverance from Egypt. Passover was also the beginning of the religious year for Israel (Ex. 12:2), and the Lord chose that significant day to tell His servant about the glory that Israel would share when Messiah established His kingdom.

In a vision, Ezekiel visited the land of Israel, but unlike his previous visits, he didn't see sinful people, a devastated land, or a defiled temple. This time he saw a new land and a glorious new temple. Just as Moses received the tabernacle plans while on a mountain, so Ezekiel received the plans for the temple while on a mountain. Moses wasn't allowed to enter the Promised Land, but he saw it from a mountain (Deut. 34:1–4), and from a high mountain Ezekiel saw the land and its new tribal divisions.

—*Be Reverent*, page 220

8. Review Ezekiel 40:1—46:24. Why was it significant that Ezekiel's vision and Moses' receipt of the tabernacle plans both occurred on a "high mountain"? What is the symbolism of the mountain in these visions? What are other ways Scripture uses the image of mountains to make a spiritual point?

More to Consider: In both the tabernacle and the temple, God's glory was "enthroned" on the mercy seat in the Holy of Holies (Ex. 25:22; Ps. 80:1; 99:1), but the millennial temple will have no ark and no mercy seat. However, the temple will still be God's throne (Ezek. 43:6–7), and the Messiah will reign as both king and priest (Zech. 6:9–13). Read Hebrews 6:20 and Psalm 110:1–4. What do these verses reveal about Jesus' role as our high priest? Why is it important to understand this role in the context of the Old Testament high priests?

From the Commentary

> The closing chapters of Ezekiel's prophecy explain how the land of Israel will be divided during the kingdom age, with a section assigned to the Lord, another to the prince, and then one to each of the twelve tribes. The first assignments of the Promised Land were made after the conquest of Canaan, with Joshua, Eleazar the high priest, and the heads of the twelve tribes casting lots before the Lord to determine the boundaries (Num. 26:52–56; 34:16–29; Josh. 13—22). During his reign, King Solomon divided the land into twelve "royal districts," and required each district to provide food for the king and his household for one month (1 Kings 4:7–19), but no actual boundary lines were changed. However, the plan wasn't popular with the people (1 Kings 12:1–19).

> —*Be Reverent*, page 230

9. Why was it important for God to explain the division of Israel's land during the kingdom age? How would that have provided some sense of peace and clarity to the exiled people? Why do we long for clarity and explanation of God's plans? What does that say about us? What does God's delay in sharing the details about His future with today's church say about His character?

From the Commentary

> In examining all the information Ezekiel recorded for
> us, we must be careful not to lose the major messages
> among these important details. There is a sense in which
> the messages of the entire book are wrapped up in one
> way or another in chapters 40 through 48. The spiritual
> lessons are as meaningful to us today as they were to Israel
> in Ezekiel's day, or as they will be to the Jewish people in
> Messiah's day.
>
> —*Be Reverent*, page 236

10. What are the lessons we can learn from the book of Ezekiel about each
of the following issues: separation from sin; worship; fulfillment of God's
promises; God's glory and God's name; God's sovereign rule? How does
this book give us hope for the church today? What practical lessons can
we take from all that Ezekiel shared with the exiled Jews? How is this a
testament to God's creativity in teaching His people across time what it
means to follow Him?

Looking Inward

Take a moment to reflect on all that you've explored thus far in this study of Ezekiel 38—48. Review your notes and answers and think about how each of these things matters in your life today.

> *Tips for Small Groups: To get the most out of this section, form pairs or trios and have group members take turns answering these questions. Be honest and as open as you can in this discussion, but most of all, be encouraging and supportive of others. Be sensitive to those who are going through particularly difficult times, and don't press for people to speak if they're uncomfortable doing so.*

11. In what ways do you see God's greatness in your life? Where does God's power intersect with your daily life? Why is it important to know and respect God's greatness? How can trusting God's power help you grow your faith?

12. What does holiness mean to you? How do you honor God's holiness in your life? What about God's holiness inspires you? Challenges you? How can you learn to be more reverent in your worship?

13. What is your greatest hope today? How might God answer that hope now or in the near future? How can you live in the tension that God may choose not to answer your hope today but rather in the world to come? What are the challenges of seeking God's immediate action in your life? How does trust play into your approach to God in these areas of need or concern?

Going Forward

14. Think of one or two things that you have learned that you'd like to work on in the coming week. Remember that this is all about quality, not quantity. It's better to work on one specific area of life and do it well than to work on many and do poorly (or to be so overwhelmed that you simply don't try).

Do you want to be more intentional in celebrating God's greatness or holiness? Be specific. Go back through Ezekiel 38—48 and put a star next to the phrase or verse that is most encouraging to you. Consider memorizing this verse.

> *Real-Life Application Ideas: This week, focus your worship on God's sovereignty. Take a moment to consider all the people in your world—friends, family, coworkers, leaders, etc.—and the challenges they face. God may choose to solve some of their issues soon (and He may even use you to do that), but He may decide to use those difficult times for other purposes, which might make little sense to us today but have their reasons in God's economy. As you worship this week, invite God's action to help those in need today, but also thank Him for being in control of the big picture and for showing up at just the right time in just the right place. Then practice trusting God in all things as you go forward from here.*

Seeking Help

15. Write a prayer below (or simply pray one in silence), inviting God to work on your mind and heart in those areas you've noted in the Going Forward section. Be honest about your desires and fears.

Notes for Small Groups:

- *Look for ways to put into practice the things you wrote in the Going Forward section. Talk with other group members about your ideas and commit to being accountable to one another.*

- *During the coming week, ask the Holy Spirit to continue to reveal truth to you from what you've read and studied.*

Summary and Review

Notes for Small Groups: This session is a summary and review of this book. Because of that, it is shorter than the previous lessons. If you are using this in a small-group setting, consider combining this lesson with a time of fellowship or a shared meal.

Before you begin ...
- *Pray for the Holy Spirit to reveal truth and wisdom as you go through this lesson.*
- *Briefly review the notes you made in the previous sessions. You will refer back to previous sections throughout this bonus lesson.*

Looking Back

1. Over the past eight lessons, you've examined the book of Ezekiel. What expectations did you bring to this study? In what ways were those expectations met?

2. What is the most significant personal discovery you've made from this study?

3. What surprised you most about the book of Ezekiel? What, if anything, troubled you?

Progress Report

4. Take a few moments to review the Going Forward sections of the previous lessons. How would you rate your progress for each of the things you chose to work on? What adjustments, if any, do you need to make to continue on the path toward spiritual maturity?

5. In what ways have you grown closer to Christ during this study? Take a moment to celebrate those things. Then think of areas where you feel you still need to grow and note those here. Make plans to revisit this study in a few weeks to review your growing faith.

Things to Pray About

6. Ezekiel is a book about reverence and trust. As you reflect on these themes, ask God to teach you how to trust Him and to show Him proper honor in all that you do—in relationships, in work, and in worship.

7. The messages in Ezekiel include believing in God's sovereignty, seeking hope, honoring God, trusting God's promises, and learning to wait on God. Spend time praying about each of these topics.

8. Whether you've been studying this in a small group or on your own, there are many other Christians working through the very same issues you discovered when examining the book of Ezekiel. Take time to pray for them, that God would reveal truth, that the Holy Spirit would guide you, and that each person might grow in spiritual maturity according to God's will.

A Blessing of Encouragement

Studying the Bible is one of the best ways to learn how to be more like Christ. Thanks for taking this step. In closing, let this blessing precede you and follow you into the next week while you continue to marinate in God's Word:

May God light your path to greater understanding as you review the truths found in the book of Ezekiel and consider how they can help you grow closer to Christ.

The "BE" series . . .

For years pastors and lay leaders have embraced Warren W. Wiersbe's very accessible commentary of the Bible through the individual "BE" series. Through the work of David C Cook Global Mission, the "BE" series is part of a library of books made available to indigenous Christian workers. These are men and women who are called by God to grow the kingdom through their work with the local church worldwide. Here are a few of their remarks as to how Dr. Wiersbe's writings have benefited their ministry.

"Most Christian books I see are priced too high for me . . .
I received a collection that included 12 Wiersbe
commentaries a few months ago and I have
read every one of them.
I use them for my personal devotions every day and they
are incredibly helpful for preparing sermons.
The contribution David C Cook is making to the
church in India is amazing."

—Pastor E. M. Abraham, Hyderabad, India

Get the Entire
Fifty-Book "BE" Series
in Two Volumes

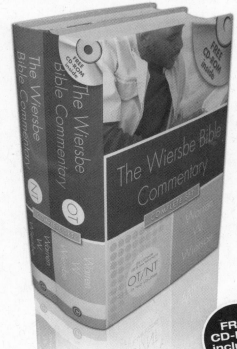

FREE
CD-ROM
included

The Wiersbe Bible Commentary

Here in two volumes is all the exciting, life-changing truth of the Scriptures wrapped in the warm, personal wisdom of one of America's best-known Bible teachers, Dr. Warren W. Wiersbe. *The Wiersbe Bible Commentary* helps you study the entire Bible in easy-to-read sections that emphasize personal application as well as biblical meaning.

ISBN: 978-0-7814-4541-2

To learn more visit our Web site or a Christian bookstore near you.